CREATING HIGH-QUALITY CLASSROOM ASSIGNMENTS

Lindsay Clare Matsumura

ScarecrowEducation
Lanham, Maryland • Toronto • Oxford
2005

Published in the United States of America
by ScarecrowEducation
An imprint of The Rowman & Littlefield Publishing Group, Inc.
4501 Forbes Boulevard, Suite 200, Lanham, Maryland 20706
www.scarecroweducation.com

PO Box 317
Oxford
OX2 9RU, UK

British Library Cataloguing in Publication Information Available

Library of Congress Cataloging-in-Publication Data

Matsumura, Lindsay Clare, 1966–
  Creating high-quality classroom assignments / Lindsay Clare Matsumura.
     p. cm.
  Includes bibliographical references and index.
  ISBN 1-57886-207-8 (pbk. : alk. paper)
  1. Effective teaching. 2. Learning. 3. Education—Aims and objectives. I. Title.

LB1025.3.M344 2005
371.102—dc22

                                        2004024678

∞^TM The paper used in this publication meets the minimum requirements of
American National Standard for Information Sciences—Permanence of
Paper for Printed Library Materials, ANSI/NISO Z39.48-1992.
Manufactured in the United States of America.

To John,
and for the teachers who opened up their classrooms
and generously shared their assignments

CONTENTS

FOREWORD: STEADY WORK AND CONTINUOUS PROGRESS

When you improve a little each day, eventually big things occur. . . . Not tomorrow, not the next day, but eventually a big gain is made. Don't look for the big, quick improvement. Seek the small improvement one day at a time. That's the only way it happens—and when it happens, it lasts. (Wooden, 1997, p. 143)

Improving teaching is the key to improving student achievement. New standards, tests, books, and other such reforms by themselves are not enough. Teaching is the final common pathway for virtually all educational reforms. To make a real difference, we have to change the *way* teachers teach. Changed teaching is the true measure of reform. But changing teaching is the hardest aspect of implementing reform. Happily, more reformers are avoiding the major miscalculations of their predecessors who assumed teaching changes could be made quickly and easily. More and more, people realize that change is very difficult and that fast solutions don't work.

Education professionals are beginning to accept Coach Wooden's advice that *steady work and continuous improvement* are the best ways to change teaching. It's a lesson he learned as a high school English teacher, long before he was named the greatest coach of the twentieth century. Over the course of 11 years, his UCLA teams won 10 national championships. Yet throughout his career he insisted that much of what he knew about coaching he learned as a high school English teacher in the 1930s. He often says he just carried over to the court lessons learned in the classroom (Gallimore & Tharp, 2004). And one of the most important of those lessons was the power of steady work and continuous improvement.

Some improvements require fundamental changes in the everyday routines of public schools, including time for teachers to work collaboratively, identifying stable settings in which teachers can get classroom-focused work done (Goldenberg, 2004), turning standards into day-to-day learning goals for students, and giving teachers the opportunity to plan lessons that teach to these goals, construct assessments of what students are learning (or not learning), use learning assessments as a guide for lesson planning and revision, develop quality assignments, and to see others teach and to be seen teaching (Stigler & Hiebert, 1999). All of these seem sensible enough, and there are increasing reports that they can make a major difference in teaching and student achievement.

One lesson being learned is the importance of the fitting innovation into existing teaching practices. In general, it is more effective to improve on an existing practice than to introduce a wholly new one. Why? Every practice is part of a system. Introducing new features into an existing system can have ripple effects that in turn can create waves of resistance. Not necessarily resistance to change by teachers, but the kind that is created by a complex system in which a new practice does not naturally fit. If the new practice is a poor fit, more than likely any change will be superficial and the innovation will be absorbed into and made to fit existing practices.

In this book Lindsay Clare Matsumura presents an excellent example of an innovation that builds on existing practice: evaluating classroom assignments. Every teacher creates assignments. It is an existing practice. It is a familiar one. An innovation that builds on assignment making has a very good chance of surviving and succeeding. Through her own and others' research, she documents that the quality of classroom assignments varies substantially across teachers and schools. Some teachers are doing a good job: they choose academically substantive texts, set high goals for student learning, develop challenging activities, align tasks with learning standards, and provide effective feedback to students. Not surprisingly, assignment quality matters. Students given high-quality assignments learn more and produce better end products. They score higher on standardized tests of achievement.

Improving the quality of assignments, however, is something that is not going to happen by means of a policy change or administrative fiat. Instead, as familiar as classroom assignments are, it will take steady work by teachers to achieve the benefits that Matsumura documents.

Unhappily, many promising innovations like this are never fully implemented. Teachers have seen it many times. A new idea, policy, or practice is adopted by a school district, and the reformers think, Great, the hard part's done. Teachers know better. The "hard part" is just the beginning—what has to follow is to turn the innovation into classroom practices that change what students experience and learn every day. To get changes into the classroom so students benefit, teachers have to translate, transform, and implement what's new. Far too many people who are not working teachers think that this is "no big deal."

But it is a big deal. With weary or bemused smiles, teachers recount the often very brief support they received. They'll complain that no one seems to know *how* to do what they are asked to do and that they are left to discover that part on their own, from generalized principles. What they want and need is knowledge that is detailed, concrete, and specific (Hiebert, Gallimore, & Stigler, 2002).

Don't be surprised if eyes flash in anger. "Just another flavor of the year. Chances are it will be replaced with another one next year. The experts 'blow in, blow hot, and blow out' like the wind, leaving us with a mess to clean up and no real help when we need it." The reformers, they insist, often lose interest when it gets to the nuts and bolts of making changes a part of everyday classroom routine. As one school principal put it, "If you forget about the nuts and bolts, there's a tendency for things to fall apart."

It is the nuts and bolts of improving assignment quality that this book presents. For each aspect of assignment quality Matsumura provides detailed, practical guidance and examples. The chapter titles themselves tell the tale. A teacher who reads and takes to heart the practical, tested ideas and practices in this book can improve the quality of classroom assignments and increase their students' opportunities to learn.

It takes steady work to achieve continuous improvement in assignment quality. "That's the only way it happens—and when it happens, it lasts" (Wooden, 1997, p. 143). This book gives teachers the concrete information and tools they need to make better assignments happen and achieve lasting results for their students.

Ronald Gallimore
University of California, Los Angeles

PREFACE

I first started looking at the assignments teachers gave to students as a way to understand the impact of reform efforts on students' opportunity to learn. I focused primarily on urban schools that serve an ethnically diverse body of students from low-income families. Over the years I discovered three important things about assignment quality that became the catalyst for this book.

First, assignment quality often varies a great deal from teacher to teacher, even within the same school. Despite a range of efforts across the country to foster "whole school" reform, teachers working next door to or down the hall from one another create assignments that provide very different learning opportunities for their students. Second, assignment quality makes a difference in student learning. My research and others' have shown that students produce higher-quality written work and perform at higher levels on standardized tests of achievement when they are exposed to higher-quality assignments. My colleagues and I found, for example, that the content and organization of students' written work was improved when assignments were more cognitively rigorous, the goals for student learning were clear, and the grading criteria and task were aligned with the learning goals (Aschbacher, 1999; Clare & Aschbacher, 2001). A later study showed as well that secondary students performed at higher levels on the reading subscales of the Stanford test of achievement (SAT-9) when their teacher engaged them in more cognitively challenging assignment activities. These students also had higher scores on the language subscales of the SAT-9 when their teacher engaged them in assignment activities that had clearer grading criteria. This was after controlling for students' prior level of achievement, gender, English-language proficiency, and socioeconomic status (Matsumura, Garnier, Pascal, & Valdés, 2002). These results were similar to the findings in a larger-scale study conducted by Fred Newmann, Anthony Bryk, and their colleagues at the Consortium on Chicago School Research, who found that students performed at higher levels on standardized tests of achievement when they were exposed to assignments that posed higher intellectual demands (Newmann, Bryk, & Nagaoka, 2001). This was after controlling for students' race, socioeconomic status, gender, and prior level of achievement.

Third, although assignments have the power to foster student learning, this potential is often not realized in practice. Students often are not provided with the types of assignments and relevant support that enable them to develop their academic thinking and writing skills. The question is, how does one determine the degree to which an assignment supports and guides students to develop higher-level thinking and writing skills? How can an assignment be improved so that students have a greater opportunity to learn?

This book was written to provide some answers to these questions and communicate the results of research on assignment quality to teachers—the people who most influence students' classroom learning opportunities. Specifically, this book presents rubrics, along with examples of assignments and student work from elementary, middle, and high school, to guide reflection on assignment quality from design to implementation to the assessment of student work.

Examples for each scale-point of the rubrics are provided based on assignments and student work collected from classrooms but have been substantively altered for the purposes of this book. In some cases material was added to existing work; for example, two separate grading criteria or pieces of student work were combined. In other cases, material was edited out of student work or an assignment to underscore a particular point, and to further preserve the anonymity of the teachers and students.

In the interest of clarity and brevity, this book specifically focuses on responses to literature assignments, though many of the principles described here could apply to other content areas and other genres besides fiction (e.g., nonfiction texts). I chose response to literature because these assignments bring together both reading comprehension and academic writing skills and because the ability to write meaningfully about texts is a skill that is included in most English-language-arts standards.

It is notable that the rubrics in this book are different from other rubrics I have developed and contributed to, mostly because the requirements of a psychometrically sound instrument are different than rubrics that could be used to create high-quality assignments. If one were seeking to use assignments to assess instruction in large-scale research designs, it would not be necessary—or even desirable—to use several dimensions to examine assignment quality. Other tools would be more useful for that purpose (see, for example, Clare & Aschbacher, 2001; Matsumura, Garnier, Pascal, & Valdés, 2002; Crosson, Junker, Matsumura, & Resnick, 2003; Newmann, Bryk, & Nagaoka, 2001). The rubrics in this book, however, are meant to serve as a learning tool to improve assignment quality, not to generate global evaluations of instruction. Just as individual teachers vary in their strengths and weaknesses, individual assignments vary in the ways that they might be improved. In fact, it is rare to find assignments that are of uniform good or poor quality. The multiple dimensions, or aspects, of assignments as outlined in this book are necessary, therefore, to tailor feedback to teachers' needs and provide specific suggestions for how to improve a particular assignment.

The intended audience for this book is teachers or teacher candidates and the people who support teachers' work in classrooms (e.g., literacy coaches, professional development providers, principals, and school district personnel). For people who are studying to be teachers or who are new to the classroom, this book can serve as a guide for creating and implementing assignment tasks. For example, student teachers, working with master teachers, their fellow students, or their professors, could use the rubrics to create assignment activities that they could "pilot" in classrooms as part of their student teaching experience (with the permission and blessing of the supervising teacher, of course). This could help new teachers gain experience creating assignment tasks, and assessment criteria, and providing feedback to students on their efforts, and it would provide them with experience working with others to develop classroom activities (so that they can be more effective professional collaborators in their future schools).

For more experienced teachers, this book is intended to help fine-tune existing assignments, as well as support the creation of new assignment activities. Teachers could use these rubrics on their own as a tool for self-study; however, these rubrics, and the process they outline for creating an assignment activity probably are more useful in collaborative settings. At the end of the day, reform is a whole-school enterprise. The gaps in instructional quality and student learning will not lessen in a meaningful way without teachers working together to collectively develop and implement high-quality assignments. The process of creating and implementing high-quality assignments is difficult and time-consuming, and it would be much more efficient for groups of teachers to work together to create excellent assignment activities and create or choose high-quality assessment criteria together than to engage in this process individually. This would enable multiple assignments to be developed, tried out, and refined over the course of a school year. Working in a group has the additional benefit of formalizing a way to regularly mentor and guide new teachers at a school and to support teachers who have recently been transferred from another grade level, in addition to building up a collective store of assignments at a school that support higher-quality student work and learning.

In addition to improving assignment quality, these rubrics also are intended to help teachers be more critical consumers of the assignments they obtain from commercial sources. Especially at the elementary school level, there are a wide range of published assignment materials available for teachers to use, and many teachers do provide these assignments to their students on a routine basis. In some schools, teachers draw on a variety of published materials, whereas at other schools teachers are beholden to using one published curricula. Some of these "canned" assignments are excellent, and some are of poor quality. It is my hope that the process of reflecting on assignment quality generally will inspire teachers to evaluate more objectively the published assignment materials they have at their disposal—to reject and accept these assignments on the basis of an external criteria—and not assume that commercially available assignments are high quality because they have been published.

This book also was written for the people who directly support the work of teachers. Many reform efforts have focused on the role that instructional leadership plays within a school and district. Few tools exist, however, for supporting administrators to serve as instructional leaders. This book is intended to serve as such a tool, by providing a framework for talking and thinking about assignment quality. This will help teacher supporters know what to look for in assignments and student work from their school, as well as what questions to ask teachers about those assignments.

ACKNOWLEDGMENTS

This book was made possible by the efforts of many talented people. I began looking at classroom assignments at the National Center for Research on Evaluation and Student Testing at UCLA as part of the evaluation of the Los Angeles Annenberg Metropolitan Project. I am indebted to Pam Aschbacher, who spearheaded this work, and to Joan Herman, Eva Baker, Jenny Pascal, Joan Steinberg, Rosa Valdés, Joanne Michiuye, and others who worked with me on this project. I also owe a debt of gratitude to Genevieve Patthey-Chavez and Rosa Valdés for their collaboration with me in looking at teachers' feedback to students, and to Helen Garnier and Kyung-Sung Kim, who conducted many statistical analyses. A special thank-you also to Steven Cantrell and the Program Evaluation and Research Branch of the Los Angeles Unified School District, and to Wendy McColsky and her colleagues at SERVE for seeing the potential in this work and encouraging its development.

More recently, I have looked at assignment quality at the Learning Research and Development Center at the University of Pittsburgh as part of an effort to develop a tool kit for assessing instructional quality. For their input and insights, I am indebted to my collaborators on this project: Amy Crosson, Brian Junker, Allison Levison, Maureen Peterson, Lauren Resnick, and Mikyung Wolf.

Although I am indebted to all of these people, the dimensions described in this book have been substantively revised, and many new dimensions have been added for the purposes of this book serving as a learning tool for teachers and others, as opposed to an assessment tool. Thus, any shortcomings and oversights are entirely my responsibility and do not reflect on my colleagues' work.

I owe a great deal to the people who generously read earlier versions or parts of this book and who gave me valuable feedback: Nancy Artz, Donna Bickel, Amy Crosson, Ronald Gallimore, John Matsumura, Margaret McKeown, Maureen Peterson, Lauren Resnick, and Carrie Rothstein-Fisch. And finally, I want to thank John Matsumura, Virginia Fawcett, George and Patsy Matsumura, Susan Millmann, Steve Clare, and others who babysat my infant son so I could write and finish this book.

1

CLASSROOM ASSIGNMENT QUALITY: AN INTRODUCTION

As any writer, scientist, artist, musician, or parent knows, meaningful skills can always be improved upon, even when a level of proficiency has been reached. In fact, improving skills such as these constitute a life's work. The same is true of teaching. No matter how skilled a teacher is, the quality of his or her instruction can always be refined. This book is intended to support this process of continual refinement and improvement in classroom practice by presenting a set of tools that can help teachers hone their skills at developing and implementing assignments and assessing students' work.

Assignment quality, as it is defined in this book, puts into practice powerful research-based concepts for teaching. To support teachers in developing, reflecting on, and fine-tuning the assignments they create, this book presents a series of rubrics with benchmark examples from elementary, middle, and high school classrooms. These rubrics are meant to serve as a diagnostic tool in assessing the strengths and weaknesses of an assignment, as well as to guide the creation of new assignments for students.

This is not quick and easy work. Creating a high-quality assignment involves many aspects of instruction and of student learning—from choosing texts to providing written comments on drafts of students' work.

These skills take a long time to master and can involve a certain amount of trial and error. No teacher can expect every assignment to be an unmitigated success in every way at first try. As with all meaningful skills, however, through steady work and continuous improvement assignment tasks will improve, and students' opportunity to learn will increase as a result.

The following sections outline the basic steps that are part of creating a high-quality assignment, specifically with regard to responding to literature. The rubrics used to analyze assignment quality also are described, as well as what a teacher would need to do to begin the analysis process.

CHOOSING AN ACADEMICALLY SUBSTANTIVE TEXT

The first step in developing a high-quality assignment is to choose the right text for students. For content areas that are not necessarily text based, such as math or science, this could mean choosing the right activity or problem for students to solve. For literature assignments, the right text is one that has enough thematic or plot complexity, or complexity in the language or imagery used by an author, to support meaningful classroom discussions and written responses (Beck, McKeown, Hamilton, & Kucan, 1997). A predictable plot with shallow characters, for example, would not support interesting assignments, as there would be little nonobvious content to comprehend, think about, or write about. The text, of course, also should be appropriate for the age of the students. A text that is engaging for elementary school students, for example, would likely not be interesting to middle school–age children, even if these students were reading on an elementary school level.

ANALYZING A TEXT BEFORE DISCUSSING IT WITH STUDENTS

The next step is to analyze the text and to decide what students should learn or comprehend from the story (or the sections of a story in a longer chapter book). What are the meaningful themes? What is the primary conflict in the story? What was the author's purpose in writing the story? Reading the assigned texts with other teachers, or at least other adults, can be very helpful, because it can bring multiple perspectives to bear on what to focus on in a discussion and in an assignment.

SETTING CLEAR AND RIGOROUS GOALS FOR STUDENT LEARNING

After choosing and analyzing a text, the next step is to decide what students should learn as a result of completing an assignment. Developing learning goals is a complex process. For responses to literature assignments, goals ideally are built around the standards for instruction and student learning already in place within a school, the specific content students are expected to comprehend or engage with in a text, and the writing skills students need to develop. The instructional goals for an assignment also should be clear and explicit about what students are expected to learn as a result of completing the assignment and should include a focus on the development of higher-level skills (e.g., that students will understand how an author uses literary devices to further a story's theme) rather than the means by which instruction will take place (e.g., that students will draft a five-paragraph essay) (Slavin & Madden, 1989). Although it could be appropriate for some of the learning goals to emphasize basic skills (e.g., that students will use punctuation correctly in their writing and that they will be able to summarize the basic events in a story) at least some of the goals should focus on students developing the ability to analyze and interpret what they read and improve their academic writing skills.

DEVELOPING THE ASSIGNMENT TASK

The next step in creating an assignment is to design or choose a task that furthers the learning goals. As described earlier, the assignment should provide students with an opportunity to apply higher-level comprehension skills (that is, analyze and interpret a text) in the service of truly understanding what they read and to provide evidence from a text to support their assertions. A great many cognitive operations are needed to comprehend text. These include mental procedures that allow readers to decode printed words and build a mental model or representation of the text's content. Readers also, however, need to be able to construct meaning beyond what is represented on the written page—or beyond the surface-level features of a text. The direct teaching of basic skills needs to be balanced, therefore, with the opportunity to construct meaning or develop higher-level cognitive skills (Newmann, Marks, & Gamoran, 1996; Slavin & Madden, 1989; Snow, 2002).

Higher-order thinking, also referred to as independent symbolic thinking, is characterized by the manipulation of information and ideas or "arriving at conclusions that produce new meanings or understandings" (Newmann, Marks, & Gamoran, 1996, p. 289). These skills can be developed, for example, in activities in which students apply information to new contexts (e.g., solve a problem for which there is more than one solution), construct arguments, or consider alternative perspectives (Bloom, 1956). Higher-level thinking also can be evidenced when a student analyzes a text and links the constituent parts back to each other in new ways, or evaluates a text based on external criteria. For example, having students identify the main theme of a work and show how various literary devices were used to further that theme would be an example of a response-to-literature task that supports students in applying higher-order thinking skills.

Lower-order thinking, in contrast, occurs when students recite basic factual information or employ a standard, preordained rule or format. This level of thinking, characterized as *recognition* and *recall,* requires students to identify specific content verbatim and to reproduce (remember and retrieve) specific content. In the context of responding to literature, this level of thinking generally is evidenced by having students recall basic isolated facts that were explicitly mentioned in a text (e.g., the names of characters and where they lived).

DEVELOPING AND COMMUNICATING THE STANDARDS FOR HIGH-QUALITY WORK

The next step in creating an assignment activity is to develop the standards for high-quality work—that is, the criteria upon which students' work will be judged—and communicate these to students. These criteria ideally would be explicit about what students would need to do or include in their work to be successful at a task. These expectations also would be aligned with the goals for student learning and would include a focus on the content of students' work—that is, students' mastery of higher-level skills. Ideally these expectations would be communicated to students in multiple ways; for example, in rubrics or criteria charts publicly displayed in a classroom (Institute for Learning [IFL], 2002), as well as in the assignment directions given to students. Discussing models of high-quality work with students and involving students in creating these criteria and in judging their own work also are important means of communicating the standards for high-quality work to students.

PROVIDING FEEDBACK ON STUDENTS' EFFORTS

Finally, to fully realize the potential of an assignment task designed to support student learning, students need to receive feedback on their efforts. This feedback should focus on the content of students' writing—their ideas, their arguments, and the quality of the evidence they use to support their assertions. Ideally students would have access to this feedback in advance of their completing their work so that they have the opportunity to use this feedback to revise their work (Matsumura, Patthey-Chavez, Valdés, & Garnier, 2002).

Through engaging in this process—analyzing and interpreting academically substantive texts with guidance given in the form of clear and rigorous performance standards and feedback on their efforts—students can internalize the criteria for high-quality work and master these academically substantive skills.

ASSESSING ASSIGNMENT QUALITY

The specific rubrics used in this book to assess assignment quality are based on the steps already described for creating an assignment.

Engaging With Substantive Content Material

This dimension focuses on the quality of the text students read for a particular assignment. A high score for this dimension would indicate that the text contained content that was sufficiently complex to support meaningful written responses and discussion.

Setting Clear and Rigorous Goals for Student Learning

This dimension focuses on the quality of the learning goals for a particular assignment. A high score on this dimension would indicate that the learning goals for an assignment were very clear and explicit and that they focused on the development of complex thinking skills.

Applying Complex Thinking Skills: Analyzing and Interpreting Texts

This dimension focuses on the degree to which an assignment task supports students in applying higher-order thought processes to infer meaning beyond the surface-level features of a text. A high score for this dimension would indicate that students had been supported in applying complex thinking skills in the service of truly understanding a text and that they had provided substantive evidence from a text to support their responses.

Developing Clear and Rigorous Criteria to Assess Students' Work

This dimension focuses on the quality of the criteria used to grade students' work. A high score for this dimension would indicate that the criteria for grading student work were very clear and explicit and that they focused, at least in part, on students applying complex thinking skills in the service of analyzing and interpreting a text.

Communicating the Criteria for High-Quality Work to Students

This dimension focuses on how the performance expectations (specifically the grading criteria) are communicated to students. A high score for this dimension would indicate that the criteria for high-quality work were communicated to students in a range of ways and that students had the opportunity to apply these criteria to their own work.

Providing Clear and Rigorous Written Assignment Directions

This dimension focuses on the quality of the performance expectations as they are communicated in the written assignment directions provided to students. A high score for this dimension would indicate that the directions were very explicit, especially with regard to students analyzing and interpreting a text.

Providing Content-Specific Feedback on Drafts of Student Work

This dimension focuses on the quality of the comments teachers provide to students on drafts of their written work. A high score for this dimension would indicate that the comments and edits provided to students on drafts of their work focused on their attainment of academic skills and content knowledge.

Aligning the Goals for Student Learning With the Assignment Task

This dimension focuses on the degree to which the goals for student learning are furthered through the assignment task. A high score for this dimension would indicate that the learning goals and the requirements for the assignment task overlapped completely.

Aligning the Assessment Criteria With the Goals for Student Learning

This dimension focuses on the degree to which the goals for student learning are included in the teacher's criteria for high-quality work. A high score for this dimension would indicate that students were assessed on the specific skills and content a teacher intended for them to master through completing the assignment task.

GETTING STARTED

The rubrics described here are probably best used in collaborative professional-development settings for teachers, though they could be used to self-assess and/or guide the development of assignments for individuals as well. If these rubrics are used to analyze the specific strengths and weaknesses of an assignment, some questions about an assignment should be answered before a teacher begins this process, and some materials should be gathered. The questions that need to be answered are as follows:

- What were students asked to do for this assignment? What activities did students complete? How were they prepared? How long did it take for students to complete the assignment?
- What were the goals for student learning? What skills and concepts were students expected to learn as a result of completing the assignment? How does the assignment fit with the school's standards for instruction and student learning? (Remember to be as specific as possible.)
- What directions were given to students? Did students receive a written copy of the directions? (If so, include these with the other materials.)
- What were the criteria for grading student work? Was a rubric or criteria chart used to assess student work? (If so, include a copy with the other assignment materials. If not, write down the criteria that were used to determine the difference between low-, medium-, and high-quality student work.)
- How were the assessment criteria shared with students? Were the criteria discussed with students in class? Was there a public record of the criteria students could refer to (e.g., a posted criteria chart, a rubric that was distributed for students to refer to when completing the assignment)? Did students see a model of high-quality work? Did they participate in setting the criteria?

In addition to answering these questions, a teacher also would need to choose samples of students' work (of high, medium, and low quality) for that assignment. The reason for looking at samples of student work is to better understand the assignment as well as to reflect on how specific changes in the assignment might yield higher-quality student work. If the assignment required students to write multiple drafts, each sample should include the entire set of drafts in order to show how the students' writing improved across drafts and to demonstrate the type and amount of feedback provided to students to guide their revisions.

Once these materials and information have been gathered, the assignment is ready to be analyzed. The chapters that follow provide descriptors for each of the dimensions of quality. Examples of assignments and student work are provided for grades 3, 7, and 10 to illustrate each of the scale points, and questions are included at the end of each chapter to guide reflection and analysis. To determine a scale point for a particular dimension, the example that is closest to the targeted grade should be chosen. For example, a sixth-grade teacher should look at the seventh-grade examples, a high school teacher should look at the tenth-grade samples, and so forth.

Finally, it is important to keep in mind that the end goal of engaging in this process is to generate specific ideas for how to strengthen an assignment—to make it more challenging and aligned with standards and/or more supportive of student learning. To this end, it is important to look at each dimension carefully and not to let the perception of one dimension prejudice the perception of another. For example, it is common when people are rating something (e.g., student work and test questions) to allow their judgment of overall quality color their ratings of individual dimensions; in other words, for there to be a halo effect. To avoid this, each dimension should be considered independently. As described earlier, an assignment that is strong overall might still have aspects that could be improved, and an assignment with many weaknesses could still have areas of strength.

2

CHOOSING THE RIGHT TEXT

Choosing the right text lies at the heart of creating excellent responses to literature assignments. As all teachers and students know, texts can be either easy or difficult to understand, depending on the subject matter, the complexity of the linguistic structures used (e.g., complexity of syntax and sentence structure), and difficulty or specialization of vocabulary. Simply choosing a text that is matched to students' reading abilities, however, is not enough to create an excellent assignment. It is necessary as well that texts contain ideas and themes that are complex enough to support meaningful discussions and written responses. It also is important that texts be appropriate to the age and interests of the students—regardless of their reading level. Books that contain surface-level characters and predictable, formulaic plot lines, for example, will not provide the material needed to develop analysis and interpretation skills, because there is little in these stories that is nonobvious and that would require analysis and interpretation.

This way at looking at the content of texts has been referred to as "grist" by Isabel Beck and Margaret McKeown (2001), nationally recognized experts in reading comprehension and vocabulary instruction. Beck and McKeown found that a text's level of grist was an important precursor to effective literacy instruction that enhances students' language development. While their research focused on the quality of book discussions with primary-grade students, the idea of grist could translate just as well to older students writing about what they had read.

In this book, texts that are considered to contain sufficient grist to support a meaningful conversation and writing task would have at least some (not necessarily all) of the following characteristics:

- A message that transcends the actual events portrayed on the page,
- A complex, unpredictable plot line,
- A moral dilemma that does not have an obvious right or wrong answer,
- Characters that are neither all good nor all bad, and that develop or change in some way over the course of the story.

Charlotte's Web by E. B. White (1952) is an excellent example of a book for young students that illustrates these dimensions of grist. This book is about a spider, Charlotte, who weaves messages in her web above her pig friend Wilbur's pen, to save him from being slaughtered. This book contains an important message about selflessness and love. The story line, which unfolds over several chapters, is quite complicated and describes the development of the main character and his friendships with others. The story events are not predictable. For example, at the beginning of the story, when Wilbur's life is first saved by a young girl, there is no way for the reader to know that his life will later be saved by a spider who shares his pen, nor is it clear how the story will end. This book also contains an interesting moral dilemma and multidimensional characters. For example, Mr. Zucherman's decision to butcher Wilbur provides the central crisis in the story. Casting him solely as a villain, however, does not do justice to his character: he is a farmer who is doing his job to provide for his family. The rat, Templeton, is another complex character who provides invaluable assistance to Wilbur but exacts a price for his help, in contrast to the selfless love shown by Charlotte.

Grist can also be seen in the complexity of the writer's craft; for example, in the language use, vocabulary, and organizational structures employed by an author. For high school students, Shakespeare's works—with their poetic imagery, metaphor, use of iambic pentameter, sonnet structures, and complex vocabulary—would be a good example of grist provided by the language itself.

In addition to developing students' thinking skills, the texts they read ideally would also broaden their knowledge of the world. A text that contains sufficient grist to support meaningful responses to a literature assignment, therefore, might also contain information that is relevant to another content area besides English language arts. For example, students could read literature that supports the investigation of a specific historical period, such as *Ann Frank: The Diary of a Young Girl* when learning about the Holocaust or books from the Golden Mountain Chronicles series by Laurence Yep if studying immigration or California history.

Of course, finding books that contain sufficient grist for students who are reading below grade level can be very challenging. This is a tremendous problem in many schools that serve students from low-income families and students who are English-language learners. It is not unusual for seventh graders in urban schools to read at a fourth-grade level. Finding texts that are both engaging for adolescents and "readable" at a fourth-grade level is not an easy task, and, obviously, asking students to read texts independently that are too difficult for them can frustrate and even alienate them. While it is beyond the scope of this book to fully explore this issue (that could be a book in itself), one strategy some teachers use to get around this problem is to read books (or portions of a book) aloud to students while they follow along. Preteaching for complex vocabulary, or vocabulary that is likely to be unfamiliar to nonnative speakers of English also can support students in reading difficult texts.

While other strategies doubtless exist for supporting students in reading texts that are age appropriate but beyond their reading level, the point here is that students need exposure to complex ideas in what they read in order to develop their ability to analyze. This, of course, would not take the place of direct instruction in reading for those students who need it at any grade. Confining reading comprehension to simple texts that contain only straightforward, surface-level information, however, will not provide students with the opportunity to develop higher-level academic skills, simply because there would not be much content for them to comprehend. Students cannot practice engaging with deeper-level meanings of a text if none exists. While more straightforward texts can sometimes be appropriate for building decoding skills and fluency, they generally are not as helpful for building students' academic thinking and writing skills.

LEVEL 1: NO ENGAGEMENT WITH SUBSTANTIVE CONTENT

At the first level of quality students do not engage with substantive content; that is, there is little to no evidence of grist (see Table 2.1). The text does not further students' knowledge of academic subject material or contain sufficient complexity in the narrative themes to support the development of students' analysis and interpretation skills. For example, the plot may be extremely simple, the characters may be flat or one-dimensional, and either there is no dilemma or problem in the story or the dilemma or problem has an obvious solution.

Third Grade

For this assignment students read a version of "The Three Little Pigs" in their basal reader. This version is a slightly altered retelling of the classic story that is introduced to many students during the preschool years. This assignment, therefore, illustrates a score of 1 (*low*) for this dimension because this story contains very simple themes that likely are already familiar

Table 2.1   Engaging With Substantive Academic Content (Grist)

Level 1	Level 2	Level 3
The text does not contain sufficiently complex themes or ideas to support a meaningful response (e.g., the text has a very simple plot, one-dimensional characters, and straightforward dilemmas that have an obvious right or wrong answer).	The text contains some degree of thematic complexity but does not challenge students' thinking.	Students engage with substantive content. The text contains complex themes and ideas that support meaningful responses.

to students of this age. Students probably will not learn anything new by reading this story, and the thematic content does not lend itself to especially rich discussions or responses. Reading this story also will not further students' knowledge of core literature appropriate for third grade.

Seventh Grade

For this assignment students read the book *Bunnicula* by Deborah and James Howe. This story is about a family that adopts a pet bunny. This bunny, unbeknownst to anyone but the family dog, is actually a vegetable-juice-sucking Dracula. This is a fun story that is especially appealing to elementary school students. The story is geared toward younger readers and does not contain themes or situations that would challenge the thinking of adolescent readers. Additionally, the story contains no academic content. For these reasons, the assignment was considered to illustrate the lowest score, 1, for this dimension.

Tenth Grade

A short excerpt from *The House on Mango Street* by Sandra Cisneros, assigned to a tenth-grade class, also illustrates a score of 1 for this dimension. While this is an excellent book, students were only required to read a short section: a two-page chapter on how the character got her name ("My Name"). This chapter on its own does not provide enough material for students to engage in substantive analysis or interpretation. For this reason, this assignment received the lowest score for this dimension. If students had read the entire book, this assignment would have received a high score for the quality of the text.

LEVEL 2: MINIMAL ENGAGEMENT WITH SUBSTANTIVE CONTENT

At the second level of quality, students engage with some degree of substantive content (see Table 2.1). In other words, the themes and ideas with which students engage have at least a minimal level of complexity or "grist." These may be age-appropriate stories that students enjoy, but they do not further students' knowledge and would not support particularly interesting or weighty conversations or written responses. In other words, these texts may not challenge students to consider new perspectives or expose them to meaningful ideas and information. Alternatively, these texts might not be age appropriate for the readers. In other words, the texts might be of high quality but more developmentally appropriate for younger readers.

Third Grade

For this assignment, students read and summarized a chapter from a book in the Goosebumps series. These horror stories are immensely popular with young readers. Although these stories may be fun for students to read and may even inspire some students to want to read independently, they contain little that would contribute to students' world knowledge or challenge students' thinking. For this reason, this assignment was considered to illustrate a score of 2 for this dimension.

Seventh Grade

An example of a seventh-grade assignment that received a moderate score for this dimension was one in which the students read a book from a series entitled Making Out that is geared toward young adolescent readers. The series is about ten teenagers who live in the same small town in Maine. The specific book, *Two-Timing Aisha* by Katherine Applegate, that the student chose to review for this assignment focuses on a teenage girl who finds herself torn between two boys, with predictable results. The themes explored in the book—friendship, love, and romance—would be appealing and enjoyable to many adolescent readers. The dilemmas and themes in the book are fairly predictable and not complex enough to lend themselves to substantive interpretation, analysis, or thought, however. For this reason, this assignment was considered to illustrate a 2 for this dimension.

Tenth Grade

For this assignment students read the book *Farewell to Manzanar: A True Story of Japanese American Experience During and After the*

World War II Internment by Jeanne Wakatsuki Houston. This story contains a great deal of historical information about the internment of Japanese Americans and illustrates very complex family dynamics. This story is usually assigned to younger readers (most commonly in seventh grade), however, and for this reason the assignment also received a moderate score for this dimension.

LEVEL 3: FULL ENGAGEMENT WITH SUBSTANTIVE CONTENT

At the third and highest level, students engage with substantive content material that contains sufficient grist to support meaningful discussions and responses (see Table 2.1). These texts contain complex ideas or themes that have the potential to support deep thinking on the part of students and that are appropriate and relevant to their age level. Generally, these texts can be considered to contain multiple levels of meaning. For example, characters and events may symbolize larger ideas, or characters may not always say exactly what they mean (as in real life), requiring the reader to read between the lines to infer meaning. Alternatively, these texts may contain meaningful content that furthers students' knowledge in a specific subject area.

Third Grade

For this assignment students read the book *The Hundred Dresses* by Eleanor Estes. This book is about a girl, Maddie, whose best friend, a very popular, well-off, and pretty girl, leads the other students in teasing Wanda, a poorer girl in the class. This teasing eventually causes Wanda to leave the school. The story centers on Maddie's compliance, which is born of her own fears of being teased, and her guilt over not having spoken out on Wanda's behalf. This book contains a wealth of ideas and themes that could be approached from many different directions. For example, students could be prompted to explore the reasons why people single out others to be picked on. They also could explore Maddie's reasons for not defending Wanda and whether or not her gesture of goodwill toward Wanda at the end of the story was sufficient. The characters also are complex in that they are neither all good nor all bad. Maddie, for example, although she did not act in a heroic manner, is certainly a sympathetic character, and her remorse is genuine. Because of the complexity of the story's theme and characters, this assignment was given the highest score, 3, for the engagement of students with substantive content.

Seventh Grade

A seventh-grade assignment that received a high score for exposing students to substantive content material was one in which students read *Ann Frank: The Diary of a Young Girl*. This text is an important work. In addition to its eploration of many themes that pertain to adolescence (e.g., struggles with parents, the beginning of feelings of sexuality and romance), the diary also illuminates and gives a human face to the Holocaust. The text also contains a great deal of grist with regard to exploring moral issues; for example, why some people chose to hide Jews even though they were putting themselves and their families at risk, while many other people did not. This text, therefore, is both thematically complex and multidimensional and contains a great deal of information about an important historical event. For these reasons this assignment received the highest score for the exposure of students to substantive content.

Tenth Grade

At the tenth-grade level, an assignment that received the highest score for this dimension was one in which students read the play *The Crucible* by Arthur Miller. This text, which deals with fanaticism, persecution, and scapegoating has rich thematic content. This play also has the potential to teach the reader about the Salem witch hunts, as well as McCarthyism (if the instructor made that connection for the students). The ideas in the book are timeless and provide a great deal of material for reflecting on the past and present state of our society. For this reason, this text received the highest score for the engagement of students with substantive content.

SUMMARY

The reading material students engage with creates the foundation for high-quality assignments. Regardless of reading level, students need to read, either independently or with assistance, stories that challenge their thinking, broaden their knowledge, and deepen their understanding of the world. This means reading books and stories that contain themes and ideas complex enough to support meaningful conversations and academic discussions. In summary, such texts characteristically include:

1. A message that transcends the actual events portrayed on the page
2. A complex, nonpredictable plot line
3. A moral dilemma that does not have an obvious right or wrong answer
4. Characters that are neither all good nor all bad and that develop or change in some way over the course of the story
5. Complexity in the writer's craft (e.g., interesting vocabulary, poetic imagery, metaphors, and symbolism)
6. Information about other times and places (e.g., historical information or information about other cultures and societies) or that brings awareness to important social issues (e.g., homelessness, poverty, and bullying)

QUESTIONS TO GUIDE REFLECTION AND ANALYSIS ON THE TEXTS ASSIGNED TO STUDENTS

1. Does the text read by students contain complex themes or ideas? Are students given insight into a character's inner thoughts? Does the story contain an interesting moral dilemma to which there is not necessarily an obvious right or wrong answer? Are the characters in the book multifaceted (e.g., display both positive and negative traits)? What is the author's purpose in writing the story? Does the story contain meaning beyond relating a sequence of events?
2. Does the text provide students access to learning in other content areas? For example, do they have an opportunity to learn about life in other historical periods or about other cultures?

3

WHAT'S THE POINT OF THE ASSIGNMENT? SETTING GOALS FOR STUDENT LEARNING

Stephen R. Covey, the author of *The Seven Habits of Highly Effective People*, counsels that we should "begin with the end in mind" when living our lives (p. 95). This maxim also could be applied to the process of creating assignments. Specifically, after choosing a text, the next step in creating an assignment is to decide what students are to learn as a result of completing the assignment. What specific ideas from the text are they expected to comprehend? What thinking and writing skills should they learn as a result of participating in the assignment activity? How does this assignment fit with the standards for learning and instruction and larger curricula goals?

Beginning with the "end in mind" for an assignment task is important for creating activities that further student learning and for developing grading criteria that assess students' progress toward developing higher-level academic skills. In order for this to happen, however, the goals for an assignment need to be clear and focused on getting students to learn specific content or processes. Vague or very general goals will not provide much of a focus for developing assignments or grading criteria that will shed light on students' mastery of important specific content or skills. Goals for student learning, in addition to being clear and specific, should focus on standards-based academic content and the development of complex thinking skills, in addition to other, lower-level skills as needed.

Research indicates that more successful teachers tend to hold goals that emphasize conceptual understanding and more complex thinking skills. Less successful teachers, in contrast, tend to hold goals that focus on students completing activities rather than on mastering specific skills and concepts (Onosoko, 1992; Slavin & Madden, 1989). Additionally, while few if any teachers would ever assign a task from which students were expected to learn nothing, teachers vary quite a bit with regard to how specific and detailed their learning goals are for their assignment tasks. And in fact, my research indicates that it is common for teachers to hold fairly broad and nonspecific learning goals for the assignments they give to their students.

For our purposes, an assignment that achieves a high score for this dimension would have learning goals that are very clear and explicit and would focus, at least in part, on students applying complex thinking skills in the service of analyzing and interpreting a text. An assignment that illustrates the lowest score for this dimension, in contrast, would have learning goals that are vague and/or focused on nonacademic content or procedural functions such as following directions. Of course, simply holding complex-thinking skills as a goal is not a guarantee that an assignment will be academically rigorous (this is discussed further in the following chapter). It is, however, a good place to start.

Ideally the learning goals for an assignment are also aligned with district or state standards that are currently in place for English-language arts, though not all of the standards emphasized by a state or district likely focus on the attainment of higher-level thinking skills. At least some of the content standards for student learning in a specific state or district focus as well on the attainment of lower-level skills such as mastering the use of writing conventions. For example, demonstrating the proper use of punctuation and appropriate pronoun reference are both part of California's English-language-arts standards for seventh grade. These are important and necessary skills to attain, but they do not on their own further students' ability to analyze and interpret text. It would make sense, then, that teachers' goals for student learning might include both higher- and lower-level skills, though the opportunity to develop analysis and interpretation skills should be a part of all response-to-literature assignments.

LEVEL 1: GOALS ARE UNCLEAR AND/OR DO NOT FOCUS ON STUDENTS COMPREHENDING A TEXT

At the lowest level of quality, it is very difficult or even impossible to discern what skills teachers want students to learn as a result of completing an assignment task (see Table 3.1). A teacher's goals for an assignment might be quite vague, or they might be clear but not focus on students' comprehension of and response to what they had read. For example, the goals might focus on procedural functions (e.g., completing a set of activities), nonacademic content (e.g., behavior norms such as following directions), and writing conventions.

Table 3.1   Setting Clear and Rigorous Goals for Student Learning

Level 1	Level 2	Level 3	Level 4
Goals are unclear and/or do not focus on students' comprehension of a text.	Goals are broadly stated and/or the goals focus on students attaining a surface-level understanding of a text.	Goals are clear in terms of what students are to learn from completing the assignment activity. At least some of the goals focus on students analyzing and interpreting a text (e.g., inferring major themes, comparing and contrasting, and applying an external criterion to evaluate a text).	Goals are clear in terms of what students are to learn as a result of completing the assignment task. At least some of the goals focus on students analyzing and interpreting a text (e.g., inferring major themes, comparing and contrasting, and applying an external criterion to evaluate a text) but in addition, using evidence from a text to support a position.

Third Grade

For this assignment students read a short story from a basal text and answered a series of questions. The learning goal for this assignment was that students "answer each of the questions using complete sentences." This learning goal illustrates the lowest score, 1, for this dimension because the teacher did not articulate what students were to learn that would further their understanding of the story. Learning to fully answer questions in complete sentences is certainly a necessary skill to practice and master, but on its own this learning goal does not emphasize students' development of higher-level skills that would help deepen their comprehension of the text.

Seventh Grade

For this assignment students read books of their choosing and kept a reading log. The goals for this assignment were that students "read 15 minutes a day at home and keep a log of what they read." As with the third-grade example, the clarity and content of the learning goals for the assignment received a low score because the teacher only described the activities in which students were to engage as opposed to what they were to learn as a result of completing the activities. If the teacher had specified why students were to keep a reading log and had been clear about how this would support the attainment of specific higher-level skills, then this assignment would have received a higher score for this dimension.

Tenth Grade

A tenth-grade assignment that illustrates a score of 1 for the clarity and content of the learning goals was one in which students wrote an essay about a book they had read in class. The learning goal for this assignment was for students to "use their creativity in the context of writing about a book." This goal is extremely fuzzy and does not focus on specific student learning. In other words, it is not clear what content from the book (e.g., knowledge of themes, events, and characters) or processes (e.g., writing a persuasive argument) the teacher intended students to master or practice through writing their essays.

LEVEL 2: GOALS ARE BROADLY STATED AND/OR FOCUS ON STUDENTS ATTAINING A SURFACE-LEVEL UNDERSTANDING OF A TEXT

At the second level of quality, a teacher's goals are broadly stated, and/or focus on students attaining only a surface-level understanding of a text (see Table 3.1). These goals focus on the general skills teachers want students to acquire but are not specific with regard to how a specific assignment task is intended to further the attainment of these broader goals. Or, the goals focus on students' attainment of a basic understanding of a text but do not include a focus on students developing analytic and interpretation skills.

Third Grade

For this assignment students retold, in writing, a story by Tomie de Paola. The teacher's learning goals for this assignment were that students "acquire comprehension skills and develop their writing skills," very general goals. This assignment illustrates a score of 2 for this dimension, therefore, because is not clear which comprehension skills the teacher intended students to practice with the completion of this assignment or the specific content of the story students were intended to focus on in their writing.

Seventh Grade

For this assignment, which also illustrates a score of a 2 for this dimension, students answered a series of comprehension questions about a novel they had read. The teacher's goals for this assignment were to practice "critical thinking skills and analytical thinking." As in the previous example, these goals were very general and did not specify which critical thinking or analytical skills the teacher intended students to develop as a result of completing the assignment task. For example, did the teacher want students to develop their ability to evaluate a text by applying external criteria? Did she want them to analyze the particular motivations or qualities of a character? Did she want them to focus on the historical context of the novel or compare ideas in the novel to modern ways of thinking? Because the teacher did not articulate which critical or analytical skills she wanted students to develop, this assignment received only a basic score for this dimension.

Tenth Grade

A tenth-grade assignment that also illustrates a score of 2 for this dimension was one in which students wrote an essay about the life of the main character from a novel they had read in class. The learning goals for this assignment were, "completing the steps of the writing process, comprehending what they had read, using quotations, paraphrasing, and summarizing." Again, as with the examples already described, these goals are very broadly stated and do not include an emphasis on students applying complex thinking skills in the service of analyzing the text. For this reason this assignment received only a basic score for the clarity and content of the learning goals.

LEVEL 3: GOALS ARE CLEAR AND INCLUDE SOME FOCUS ON ANALYSIS AND INTERPRETATION

At the third level of quality, the goals for an assignment are clear in terms of what students are to learn as a result of completing the assignment task. Additionally, the goals include at least some emphasis on students developing their analysis and interpretation skills, though the goals do not include a focus on students using evidence from a text to support their responses (see Table 3.1).

Third Grade

For this assignment students read a chapter book and wrote a short essay explaining how the story related to their own lives. The teacher's goals for this assignment were that students "synthesize story events and connect the main theme in the story to their lives." Connecting the main theme in the story to their lives is a fairly specific goal for student learning. This assignment also received a high score for this dimension because the learning goals emphasized that students engage with less obvious aspects of the book—the main theme—in their connections rather than simply writing about any part of the story (i.e., making surface-level connections to story events). This assignment would have received an even higher score of 4 if the teacher also had included a focus on students using evidence from the story to support their answers.

Seventh Grade

The following seventh-grade assignment also illustrates a score of 3 for this dimension. For this assignment students wrote an essay describing the main character from a novel they had read in class. The teacher's learning goals for this assignment were that students "analyze characters by using context clues from the story to detect and infer their motives." This assignment received a high score for this dimension because the teacher specified what aspect of character analysis she wanted students to focus on (i.e., using context clues from a story to infer a character's motives), as opposed to simply requesting a "character analysis" (which would have scored a 2). Additionally, these goals focus on students developing more complex thinking skills and looking beyond the surface-level features of a text.

Tenth Grade

For this assignment students answered a series of comprehension questions about a play by William Shakespeare. The teacher's goals for this assignment were that students "examine cause and effect in the story, and understand how certain events set other events in motion with tragic consequences." Here, as with the examples from third and seventh grade, the teacher was specific about the aspect of the story she wanted students to learn about (the cause and effect of key plot events), in contrast to simply stating "reading comprehension" as her goal for student learning. This goal did not receive a higher score (that is, a 4) for this dimension, however, because the teacher did not

emphasize students engaging with text-based evidence in their responses.

LEVEL 4: GOALS ARE CLEAR AND INCLUDE SOME FOCUS ON ANALYSIS AND INTERPRETATION AND USING EVIDENCE FROM A TEXT

At the highest level of quality for this dimension, the learning goals are
clear and detailed with regard to what students are to learn as a result of
completing an assignment. Additionally, at least some of these goals focus on students deepening their understanding of the text they had read
through analysis and interpretation and using evidence from a text to
support their responses (see Table 3.1).

Third Grade

A third-grade assignment that received the highest score of 4 for this
dimension was one in which the teacher required the students to write
an essay comparing and contrasting characters from two stories. Her
learning goals for this assignment were

> to give students an opportunity to learn how to organize their thoughts
> about the story element of conflict for a main character. I wanted them to
> write about how the characters from two different stories (both of whom
> were orphaned) faced similar and different problems and resolved their
> conflicts, with lots of examples from the stories. I also wanted them to
> learn how to write comparison sentences, specifically, how to use words
> like "however," "but," "both" and "also" in their writing.

This assignment received the highest score for this dimension because
the goals are very specific with regard to the intended content of student
learning (i.e., the differences and similarities in the conflicts two or-
phaned characters faced and how they resolved these conflicts). These
goals also focus on having students engage with nontrivial aspects of the
story (e.g., the similarities and differences in how characters resolved
conflicts) and using evidence from the stories to support their writing.

Seventh Grade

For this assignment students read and compared myths from different cultures. The learning goals for this assignment were for

students to learn to see patterns in myths across different societies. I wanted them to be able to identify overarching similarities across myths, as well as ways in which they are different. I also wanted them to practice the five-paragraph essay format, and use lots of examples in their essays.

These learning goals illustrate the highest score for this dimension because their aims are clear and explicit and they emphasize the attainment of higher-level skills (i.e., identifying and describing similarities and differences across texts). Additionally, the goals include a focus on using evidence from the texts (i.e., "lots of examples") to support their assertions.

Tenth Grade

The learning goals for a tenth-grade assignment that also illustrates the highest score for this dimension were for

students to analyze a short story, identify literary elements such as the author's use of plot, theme, and symbolism, and explain using specific quotes and examples how these techniques furthered the story's action.

As with the seventh-grade example, these learning goals focus on very high-level cognitive processes (e.g., how the author's use of plot, theme, and symbolism furthered the story's action) that would support students in gaining a thorough understanding of the novel they had read. The goals also are quite specific and include a focus on students using evidence (e.g., specific quotes) from the novel to support their responses. For these reasons, this assignment received the highest score, 4, for the clarity and content of the learning goals.

SUMMARY

After choosing a text, the next step in creating an effective assignment is determining what content or processes the teacher intends students to learn through completing the assignment activities. This is important for developing tasks that meet specific standards and for developing tools, such as assessment criteria, that can be used to support student learning.

Learning goals should be clear and explicit with regard to what students are to learn as a result of completing an individual assignment task—in terms of both the specific content for a text and specific writing skills. Additionally, high-quality learning goals for response to literature assignments should focus, at least in part, on allowing students to develop their analysis and interpretation skills and use text-based evidence to support their written responses. Of course, as noted throughout this chapter, simply having a learning goal that focuses on the attainment of complex thinking is not in itself sufficient for creating an academically rigorous assignment. This issue will be explored further in the next chapter.

QUESTIONS TO GUIDE REFLECTION AND ANALYSIS OF THE LEARNING GOALS FOR AN ASSIGNMENT

1. What specific ideas or content from the text are students to learn as a result of completing this assignment?
2. What writing skills are students to develop as a result of completing this assignment?
3. Are the instructional goals clear and detailed?
4. How do these goals fit with the standards for learning and instruction?
5. Do at least some of the learning goals focus on students analyzing and interpreting a text (e.g., inferring major themes, comparing and contrasting, and applying an external set of criteria to evaluate a text)?
6. Do the learning goals include a focus on students using evidence from the text to support their responses?

4

CHALLENGING STUDENTS' THINKING: ANALYZING AND INTERPRETING A TEXT

Researchers have found that very often students, especially those from low-income backgrounds, lack the opportunity to develop their analysis and interpretation skills when learning how to comprehend text. Assignments, especially those from schools that serve predominantly low-income students, often guide students to recount basic, factual information about a text or to write a paragraph or essay recounting the literal content of what they read. Rarely are students required to analyze or interpret text or think beyond the literal events or facts represented on the written page (Snow, 2002).

Moreover, even when an assignment appears at first glance to require students to apply higher-level skills, the way in which this is translated in the assignment task does not always support the development of students' comprehension or thinking skills. In other words, the strategies designed to bolster comprehension or develop the upper levels of Bloom's taxonomy of cognitive demand are not always applied in meaningful ways that meet these goals. Having a third-grade student write a one- or two-sentence prediction about what they think might happen next in a story, for instance, without supporting their answers with examples is not going to develop their skills at analyzing a text. Similarly, having seventh-grade students compare and contrast characters based on their surface-level characteristics (e.g., what they look like or where they live) or produce single-sentence responses also will not develop students' understanding of the important meaning in or relevance of a text or develop their academic writing skills.

This chapter focuses on the principles underlying the creation of cognitively challenging and academically rigorous assignments. As described in the previous chapters, reading comprehension is a complex process. For a student to become a good reader he or she must master a number of interrelated skills (or cognitive operations), including the ability to attend to and decode text, create a mental representation of the text, and create meaning from the text that extends beyond the written page (i.e., apply higher-order thinking strategies in the service of analyzing and interpreting a text). In order to develop strong writing and thinking skills, students also need the opportunity to support their ideas with evidence from a text. Ideally an assignment would provide students with an opportunity to develop these skills. In other words, in a best-case scenario students would read a text with a great deal of "grist" (described in Chapter 2), and would analyze and interpret what they read and provide extensive evidence from the text to support their answers.

LEVEL 1: RECALLING ISOLATED FACTS OR WRITING ON A TOPIC THAT DOES NOT DIRECTLY REFER TO THE TEXT

At the lowest level of challenge, students are guided in the assignment task to recount isolated information that does not build up to a coherent whole (see Table 4.1). Students recall facts about a story, but these facts are relatively fragmented and do not necessarily support students' ability to develop a coherent summary of the text. Alternatively, an assignment illustrates a score of 1 for the application of complex thinking skills if students are guided to write on a topic that does not directly pertain to the text they are reading. This is illustrated in the following example from a third-grade classroom.

Third Grade

For this assignment students read *The Giving Tree* by Shel Silverstein and wrote an essay describing the things for which they were thankful. While the teacher sought to help students connect the theme of the book with their own experience of being given to, it is apparent from the students' essays, and in her directions to them, that this connection was not well forged. The students were not guided to write about the events in the story or the story's theme of selfless giving (and selfish receiving). In fact, the students would not have needed to read this story to write their essays. For this reason, this assignment illustrates a score of 1 for the application of complex thinking skills. This is a student's submission for this assignment:

Thanksgiving

I am thankful for my family that feeds me. I am thankful for my family because they take care of me and give me food like rice, beans, turkey and corn.

I am also thankful because they buy me things like pokamon [*sic*] and games. I really like it when they take me shopping.

I like to see my family cause I could eat with them. We go to the beach and have fun. We play games together.

Table 4.1   Applying Complex Thinking Skills: Analyzing and Interpreting a Text

Level 1	Level 2	Level 3	Level 4
The assignment task guides students (1) to recall isolated straightforward information or (2) to write on a topic that does not directly reference information from the text.	The assignment task guides students (1) to construct a basic summary of the text only or (2) to apply comprehension strategies at a surface level with little or no evidence from the text to support their responses.	The assignment task guides students to begin to analyze and interpret the text and support their responses with limited evidence from the text.	The assignment task guides students to fully analyze and interpret the text and support their responses with detailed evidence from the text.

Seventh Grade

An assignment also would be achieve a score of 1 for this dimension if students were required to recall only very basic, factual information about a text. This is illustrated in the following assignment, in which students read a retelling of the myth of Prometheus and how he brought fire to mortals. Students then wrote very short responses (one or two sentences) to a series of very basic questions about the story. This assignment received the lowest score for this dimension because students were required only to recall isolated, basic facts about the myth. If students had been asked to write a comprehensive retelling of the myth or analyze and interpret the content of the myth by, for example, looking at the myth's symbolism or comparing myths across societies, then this assignment would have received a higher score for this dimension. The following is work submitted by a student for this assignment.

Prometheus

1. *Why didn't humans have fire?* Humans did not have fire because they [*sic*] gods thought that humans might then be more powerful than they were.
2. *How did Prometheus steal fire?* Prometheus waited until the gods went to sleep to steal the fire.
3. *What was Prometheus' punishment for stealing the fire?* Prometheus was chained to a rock on a mountain. Every day a bird came and ate his liver.

Tenth Grade

For this assignment students read *Of Mice and Men* by John Steinbeck and similarly answered a series of questions that required them to recall specific, isolated facts about the text. These questions did not encourage students to generate a coherent, detailed summary of the story, let alone apply any degree of complex thinking skills. Students also wrote very short responses and did not include details or examples from the story. For these reasons, this assignment, too, illustrates the lowest score for this dimension. If students had been asked to write a comprehensive summary of the story, or even of a chapter of the book, or to write about the story's themes, then this assignment would have received a higher score for this dimension. The following is a student's submission for this assignment:

Of Mice and Men

Why does Curley wear a glove on his left hand? Curley wears a glove on his left hand because he wants to keep his hand soft for his wife.

Why does Curley pick on Lennie? Curley doesn't like big guys because he is small.

What does Lennie say about Curley's wife? Lennie says that she is pretty.

What is the jerkline skinner's name? What does he look like? His name was Slim and he was tall and strong.

Why does Lennie's last name make Carlson laugh? Lennie's last name is Small and Carlson laugh [*sic*] because Lennie is so big.

What does Slim have that interests Lennie? He has five puppies.

LEVEL 2: BASIC SUMMARY OF A TEXT OR APPLYING COMPREHENSION STRATEGIES AT A SURFACE LEVEL

At the next level of challenge, students are guided to create a basic summary of a text, though at a surface level. In other words, students are not asked to identify the underlying themes or ideas in a text, or describe less obvious aspects of a text such as a character's motivation or how literary devices may be used to create a specific effect. Alternatively, assignments that illustrate a score of 2 for this dimension may guide students to apply a specific comprehension strategy, but again, only require them to do this at surface level (see Table 4.1).

Third Grade

For this assignment, students summarized the story *A Chair for My Mother* by Vera B. Williams by completing a template where they described the title, author, setting, characters, plot, steps to solving the story's problem, and the solution to this problem. The assignment task guided students to focus on the important events in the story, though students did not have the opportunity to construct meaning about the text beyond what was represented on the written page. For example, students were not guided to synthesize the text and describe its key theme, lesson, or moral. For this reason, this assignment illustrates a 2 because of the level of complex thinking it required from students. The following is a submission of student work for this assignment.

Title: A Chair for my Mother

Author: Vera B. Williams

Setting: The story takes place in the house and in the city

Characters: The main characters are the daughter, the mother and the grandmother.

Plot: The grandmother, daughter and mom did not have enough money to buy a new armchair and they needed an armchair because the old one got burned.

Steps to solve the problem: They saved the money buy [*sic*] saving the change on a big jar. The daughter saved her money by helping work at the Blue tile diner. The mom got her money by working in the blue tile diner. The grandmother got her money by saving her change after buying food.

Solution: They traded the change for ten dollar bills then they bought the armchair.

Seventh Grade

An assignment also illustrates a score of 2 for the application of complex thinking skills if students were required to apply reading comprehension strategies at surface level. This is exemplified in the following assignment, for which students read the short story "The Treasure of Lemon Brown" by Walter Myers, completed a chart that summarized the main points of the story, generated questions about the text, and predicted what they thought would happen next. While making predictions and generating questions about the text are recommended strategies for deepening reading comprehension, the way in which this was implemented in practice did not appear to provide students with much of an opportunity to develop a deeper understanding of the text. Students' responses, even those students whose work was considered to be of high quality for the class, were mostly shallow. Their predictions and questions focused on surface-level, obvious features of the text. Additionally, students were not guided to support their predictions and questions with examples from the story, and the chart they were asked to complete provided them with little space to develop their responses. For these reasons, this assignment only received a 2 for this dimension. The following is a submission of student work for this assignment considered by the teacher to be of high quality for the class.

"The Treasure of Lemon Brown"

Summary: Greg's father wanted him to get good grades. Because he was doing bad in math, his father told Greg that he could not play on the basketball team. So Greg went to an abandoned tenement. Greg was threatened by a man in the tenement. He said his name was Lemon Brown. Then they here [*sic*] are a couple of bad street men.

They come in trying to get Lemon Brown's treasure, but Lemon fought them. Lemon Brown showed Greg the treasure. It was a harmonica and newspaper clippings of him playing the piano.

Questions: What is the treasure that he has? What makes him such an important person to have a whole story named after him? Is that Lemon Brown in the picture? Why is the picture split into day and night? Why is Lemon Brown talking with him? They don't know each other. What is to happen to Lemon? Will the thugs come back? How was Jesse killed? Did Lemon really think the clippings were worth the fight?

Predictions: I think the story is about a black man trying to survive in the city. I think the black guy is a cool musician. He makes good money and isn't very old. I think he lives in a very crowded area that has a lot of pollution. It is always busy and he wants to get away from the people. I think Lemon Brown will begin again to sing the blues. Or else I think Greg will be the one singing and Lemon Brown will teach him.

Tenth Grade

For similar reasons, the following assignment received a 2 for the way it had students apply complex thinking skills. For this assignment students read *Farewell to Manzanar: A True Story of Japanese American Experience During and After the World War II Internment* by Jeanne Wakatsuki Houston and wrote an essay in which they were supposed to analyze one of the main characters (the father of the protagonist). To assist students, the teacher pointed out the specific pages of the novel that described this character. While analyzing a character would seem to be a high-level task, the way in which this was carried out for this assignment really only required students to recount basic, surface-level story events involving the father. In other words, students did not have to actually construct any new information about the father to write their essays, they simply recalled what had already been written about him in the story. For this reason this assignment received a basic score for this dimension. This assignment would have received a higher score if, for example, the students had been guided to write about specific actions of the character and how they revealed his motives, or how his relationship with the protagonist had changed over time, citing substantive evidence from the text. The following is an excerpt from a student's essay considered by the teacher to be of high quality for this assignment for this class.

Papa Wakatsuki

Papa Wakatsuki is one of the main characters in the true story "Farewell to Manzanar." He is the father of the main character, Jeanne who wrote the book. He was born in Japan and then moved to America. Big changes in his demeanor happened when he spent 9 months in Fort Lincoln. . . .

    When he returned to Fort Lincoln after nine months you could see how much he had changed during that time. His character and personality were not the only things that changed, but physically he looked like he had aged 10 years. Shortly after that papa became violent with his family. Whenever his daughter Jeanne wanted to talk to him about his experience in Fort Lincoln he would really just try and avoid saying anything.

LEVEL 3: EMERGING ANALYSIS AND INTERPRETATION OF THE TEXT

At the next highest level of challenge students are guided to analyze and interpret a text, albeit with some limitations. Although the assignments are structured to get students to construct, to some extent at least, knowledge from the text and engage with less obvious meanings or nuances of the text, the amount and type of evidence teachers require from students to support their answers may be lacking (see Table 4.1). This is illustrated in the examples that follow.

Third Grade

For this assignment students read *Beezus and Ramona* by Beverly Cleary and wrote a short essay answering the following questions: "If Beezus planned to have a parade for her birthday, how would it be different from Ramona's parade? How would it be the same?" These are interesting questions that require students to use their knowledge of the personality differences between the two sisters, Beezus and Ramona, in order to construct a response that would be consistent with the events described in the book. In contrast to writing a literal summary, this prompt does not lend itself to one right answer, though some responses could be more aligned with the behaviors of the characters than others.

While this question guides students to apply higher-order thinking skills, the teacher who gave this assignment did not guide students to use examples of prior events in the story to justify their answers. This was apparent both from the written directions to students and in the student work (even for those students considered by the teacher to have produced high-quality work), because students used only limited evidence from the texts to support their answers. For this reason, this assignment was rated a 3 instead of a 4. The following is a submission of student work for this assignment:

Beezus and Ramona

If Beezus had a parade it would be different because it would have older kids. Beezus would be more organized. They would wear costumes and carry flags and they would go outside. The kids would be more quiet and they wouldn't run around the house. Beezus would have food and things to drink for them and a birthday cake. If Ramona came and messed up Beezus's parade then Beezus would be very angry. Beezus would not have a lot of fun that day.

Seventh Grade

An assignment also is considered to illustrate a score of 3 for this dimension if students apply strategies and construct knowledge, albeit at a beginning level. In other words, as with the previous example, some part of the assignment might require students to apply complex thinking skills, though students might not go into much depth in their analyses.

This is exemplified in the following assignment, drawn from a seventh-grade class. For this assignment students read the book *Beowulf: A New Telling* by Robert Nye and wrote a five-paragraph essay comparing and contrasting the four monsters in the story. While describing the similarities and differences between the monsters requires students to construct knowledge to some degree at least, students were not guided to describe the monsters much beyond their physical descriptions. In other words, students, even those who produced essays considered by the teacher to be of high quality, were not guided by the structure of the assignment to explore much beyond the surface-level features of the monsters in their essays. This assignment would have received a higher score if students also had engaged with deeper, underlying meanings of the text by, for example, comparing the monster's symbolic meaning or the different ways the monsters may have contributed to Beowulf's development as a hero. The following is an excerpt from a student's essay considered by the teacher to be of high quality for this assignment for this class.

Beowulf and the Four Monsters

The book, "Beowulf: A New Telling" has Beowulf, the hero, battling four monsters. These are, in order of appearance, Grendel, "She" or Grendel's mother, the Four-Headed Dragon, and the Firedrake. . . .

Three of the four monsters guarded treasure. The only monster who didn't was Grendel. But Grendel had the worst breath of the four monsters. The Firedrake and the Four-Headed Dragon both spit fire. The Four-Headed monster was the only dragon that had four heads that could do different things. Grendel also had blood that would melt anything. My favorite monster was Grendel. I chose him because I think he was the ugliest monster in the story.

Tenth Grade

For this assignment students read the third act of the play *Romeo and Juliet* by William Shakespeare and answered a series of comprehension questions. Some of these questions—for example, thinking about how the play might have turned out differently had Mercutio killed Tybalt in the sword fight or how the rift between Juliet and her nurse had added to the tragedy of the events—guided students to think beyond the literal events in the text and apply some degree of complex thinking skills. The structure of the assignment did not guide students to go into much detail in their responses, however, or include many text-specific references. For example, students, even those whose work was considered by the teacher to be of high quality, wrote no more than a short paragraph in response to each question. Additionally, students were not guided into engaging with the deeper meanings of the text or the writer's craft. For these reasons this assignment illustrates a 3 and not a 4 for this dimension. The following is an excerpt (the answer to one of five questions) of student work considered by the teacher to be of high quality for this assignment for this class:

> *How does the nurse offend Juliet? How does this development add to the tragedy of events that follow?* The nurse offends Juliet at the end of Act 3 when she says that Juliet should marry Paris. This development adds to the tragedy because now Juliet doesn't have anyone to trust except for Friar Lawrence and then she starts to make some bad choices which end tragically.

LEVEL 4: ANALYSIS AND INTERPRETATION OF THE TEXT WITH SUPPORTING EVIDENCE

At the highest level of the application of complex thinking skills to literature texts, students fully analyze and interpret the text they read and engage with the text's underlying meanings and themes. Students also draw on specific, relevant examples from the text to support their answers (see Table 4.1).

Third Grade

This level of quality is exemplified in the following assignment, in which students wrote a retelling of the story *Big Al* by Andrew Clements. Students were guided to include details about the story's characters, setting, plot, problem, and resolution. Students also were specifically guided to identify the main idea or theme of the story at the beginning of their essays and to indicate, at the end of their essay, whether they ever felt like Big Al. Because this assignment required students to create a coherent retelling of the story, engage with the main themes of the story, and support their answers with details from the text, this assignment was considered to illustrate a score of 4 for this dimension. The following is an excerpt from a student's essay for this assignment:

Big Al

Big Al was lonely, so he wanted to make friends. He lived in the deep blue ocean. First he tried to talk to them, but all the fish ran away because he was to [sic] big and has sharp teeth. Next he tried to cover himself with seaweed but they ran away because he still looked ugly. Then he tried to cover up with sand. He went to the other fish but some of the sand got stuck in his nose so he sneezed. All the fish ran away. Next he pretended to be with the school fish but he kept bumping into the fish so they all ran. . . .

The theme of the story is having friends, and the outside doesn't count only the inside is what really counts. Big Al was just like me in this school because I didn't have any friends. Danny, Juan Carlos and Rene was my first friends I had at this school.

Seventh Grade

A seventh-grade assignment that also was considered exemplary for the application of complex thinking skills was one in which students read the play *A Man for All Seasons* by Robert Bolt and wrote an essay in which they addressed the following prompts:

Write a five-paragraph essay in which you discuss how Sir Thomas More defended himself against King Henry and his administration. How does the way he defends himself differ from the way traditional heroes defend themselves? Make sure to include several examples from the text to support your argument.

These prompts guided students to think about the play beyond surface-level events. Additionally, thinking abstractly about how the main character differed from traditional heroes required the students to construct knowledge about the text that went beyond recalling story events and details. Students also were guided to support their responses with text-specific examples (though some students included more examples than others). For these reasons, this assignment illustrates the highest score for this dimension. The following is an excerpt of student work for this assignment:

Sir Thomas More: An Unconventional Hero

Most people use weapons to defend themselves like swords, daggers, or catapults. Sir Thomas More knew how to get out of difficult situations, but he mainly followed his conscience. When Sir Thomas More got into difficult situations he would use other weapons to try and get himself out of it. These weapons were silence, topic changing, and his belief in God.

Sir Thomas More used the weapon of silence when King Henry VIII wanted to divorce Catherine of Aragon and marry someone else. King Henry wanted everyone to think that this was right. Everyone said that this was fine because they didn't want the king to be mad with them. Everybody agreed except Sir Thomas More. He wouldn't say why he didn't agree either. This cost him his life.

Tenth Grade

For this assignment students read *The Yellow Wallpaper* by Charlotte Perkins Gilman and wrote an essay in which they described how specific literary elements and techniques such as plot, character, symbol, irony, and so forth worked together to enhance and support the story's theme. Students were told that their essays should be at least six paragraphs in length and that they needed to include supporting quotes from the text. This assignment illustrates the highest score for the application of complex thinking skills because it was structured to get students to consider not just the theme and underlying meaning of the text but also how specific literary devices such as symbolism were used to further the story's meaning. Students, therefore, were guided to consider not just the content of the story but the writer's craft in furthering the story's theme. The following is an excerpt from a student's essay considered by the teacher to be of high quality for this assignment for this class:

"The Yellow Wallpaper" is rich in symbolism. One major symbol is the yellow wallpaper in the room where the narrator lives. It is symbolic of the restrictions put on her by her husband. Within the wallpaper she begins to see images of women being strangled which probably represent other women who are controlled by their husbands. She says, "Nobody could climb through the pattern, it strangles so, I think that is why it has so many heads." . . . The author's use of symbolism aides the reader in understanding the theme of confinement and how this leads to insanity.

SUMMARY

Ideally assignments provide students with the opportunity to develop their skills at analyzing and interpreting a text and guide students to support their answers with text-based evidence. At the lowest level of quality for this dimension, students are guided to recall basic, isolated facts about a text or to write on a topic that is only tangentially related to a text read by students. At the next level of quality, students construct a basic summary of what they read (the story events), or apply comprehension strategies at a very basic level without support from a text. At the higher levels of challenge students analyze and interpret a text, and at level 4 (*highest*) use extensive evidence from the text to support their answers.

QUESTIONS TO GUIDE REFLECTION AND ANALYSIS OF STUDENTS' OPPORTUNITY TO APPLY COMPLEX THINKING SKILLS

1. What skills do students need to apply to complete this assignment (e.g., recall of facts, summarization, evaluation, and analysis)?
2. Do students need to have a thorough understanding of the events and interrelationship of events in the text to complete this assignment? Was this reflected in the high-, medium-, and low-quality student work?
3. Do students need to have a thorough understanding of the nonobvious features of the text (e.g., the theme, the message of the text, a character's motivation, literary symbolism, and historical context) to complete this assignment? Was this reflected in the high-, medium-, and low-quality student work?
4. Did the assignment guide students to support their responses with detailed evidence from the text? Was this reflected in the high-, medium-, and low-quality student work?

5

CREATING AND COMMUNICATING THE CRITERIA FOR EXCELLENT WORK

As any educator knows, high-quality work from students depends on more than simply being assigned an academically rigorous task. Teaching would be a much simpler endeavor if this were not the case! Instead, students need support and guidance at every stage of the assignment process. This chapter, Chapter 6, and Chapter 7 focus on the support teachers give to students through their assessment criteria, in their assignment directions, and by providing feedback to students on drafts of their written work.

The criteria a teacher uses to assess students' work can serve as a powerful tool for student learning when these criteria are clear, explicit, and focused on academically rigorous content. High-quality assessments have the potential to make teachers' expectations transparent to students and can help guide students toward meeting those standards. In fact, research indicates that the use of high-quality classroom assessment tools is associated with improved student learning (Black & Wiliam, 1998).

In this book, high-quality assessment tools (or grading criteria) are defined as those containing a great deal of information about what students should do or include in their work to be successful at a task. High-quality criteria also focus (at least in part) on the development of higher-level academic skills. This is important both for communicating the standards for high-quality work to students and for providing students with feedback on their progress toward mastering higher-level thinking and writing skills. The best grading criteria in the world, however, will not support student learning if students do not have an opportunity to use these criteria to guide and shape their work. Students' access to these criteria, therefore, is as important as their quality. For this reason, this chapter focuses on both developing and communicating the criteria for assessing students' work. These issues are discussed separately in the sections of this chapter that follow.

LEVEL I: GRADING CRITERIA ARE UNCLEAR AND/OR DO NOT FOCUS ON COMPREHENDING A TEXT

At the lowest level of clarity, it is very difficult to understand the criteria a teacher is using to assess the quality of student work. The teacher's grading criteria may be expressed in very vague terms and/or may not include a focus on students' comprehension of a text (see Table 5.1). For example, the criteria may focus on procedural functions such as finishing an assignment, correctly answering a set of questions, or completing an assignment neatly. Or, the criteria may focus on skills that are not germane to comprehension, such as writing mechanics.

Third Grade

A score of 1 for this dimension is illustrated in the following assignment. For this assignment students read a short biography of George Washington and wrote him a letter describing how their world is different from when he was alive. To assess students' work, the teachers used a rubric ranging from *unsatisfactory* to *excellent*. To obtain an *excellent* score, the assignment had to be

- On-time
- Neat
- Punctuated correctly
- Complete through both rough and final drafts
- At least two paragraphs long

Table 5.1   Developing Clear and Rigorous Criteria to Assess Students' Work

Level 1	Level 2	Level 3	Level 4
Grading criteria are unclear and/or do not focus on students' comprehension of a text.	Grading criteria are broadly stated and/or criteria focus on students attaining a surface-level understanding of a text.	The grading criteria used to assess students' work are clear and somewhat elaborated. Levels of quality may be differentiated for each criterion, but little information is provided for what distinguishes between low, medium, and high work. At least some of the criteria focus on students analyzing and interpreting a text (e.g., inferring major themes, comparing and contrasting, and applying an external criterion to evaluate a text).	The grading criteria used to assess students' work are very clear and elaborated. Each dimension or criterion for the quality of students' work is clearly articulated. Additionally, varying degrees of success are clearly differentiated. At least some of the criteria focus on students analyzing and interpreting a text (e.g., inferring major themes, comparing and contrasting, and applying an external criterion to evaluate a text) and using evidence from a text to support a position.

These criteria, while fairly clear, illustrate a score of 1 for this dimension because they focus solely on procedural outcomes (e.g., completing the work on time, completing a rough and final draft) and writing mechanics (e.g., having few punctuation and spelling errors) rather than on the development of complex thinking skills that are specific to comprehension. If this rubric had included a focus on the content students were intended to master through completing the assignment task (e.g., demonstrated knowledge of the colonial period), then this assignment would have received a higher score for this dimension.

Seventh Grade

Another assignment that illustrates a score of 1 for this dimension guided students to write a continuation of a story they had read in class. To assess students' work, the teacher used a rubric ranging from 1 (*poor*) to 4 (*excellent*). To obtain the highest score for this assignment, the students' work had to be

- Creative
- Marred by fewer than three spelling or grammatical errors
- At least one page in length

These criteria do not focus on the development of critical-thinking skills or the content of students' stories. Writing a plausible continuation of a story can be a challenging task, provided that students are held accountable for being true to the events that occurred previously in the text and to the qualities, behaviors, and motivations of the characters. These criteria provide little or no guidance to students, however, with regard to the intended plausibility of their continuations. The other criteria in this rubric focus on the length of students' responses and their command of writing mechanics. Because the first criterion was vague (i.e., it is not clear what the teacher means by "creative" versus "not creative" responses) and the criteria did not include a focus on the content of students' stories or development of their complex thinking skills, this assignment also received the lowest score for this dimension.

Tenth Grade

For this assignment students answered a series of comprehension questions about a novel they had read in class. The grading criteria for this assignment were that students "answer every single question with complete sentences." This assignment received a 1 for this dimension because these criteria focused on procedural functions (i.e., that students answer every question) and mechanics (i.e., that they use complete sentences). This assignment would have received a higher score for this dimension if the criteria had focused on the content of students' responses with regard to their ability to analyze and interpret what they had read.

LEVEL 2: GRADING CRITERIA ARE BROADLY STATED AND/OR FOCUS ON STUDENTS ATTAINING A SURFACE-LEVEL UNDERSTANDING OF A TEXT

At this level of quality the criteria used by a teacher to assess student work are stated in very general terms with no detail or elaboration. Alternatively, the content of the criteria could focus on students obtaining a surface-level understanding of a text only (see Table 5.1). Most often, the grading criteria given a 2, signifying this level of quality, are expressed in the form of a general list in which none of the specific criteria are detailed or elaborated. This is illustrated in the following examples.

Third Grade

For this assignment students wrote a research report on an animal of their choice. The grading criteria for this assignment were that they include "accurate facts about the animal, written expression, detail, and proper paragraph format." These criteria illustrate a score of 2 for this dimension because they are quite broad. It is not clear what the teacher considers to be important content for students to focus on in their essays (beyond the accuracy of the facts), and so do not provide much support to students for writing their reports. If the criteria had been specific with regard to what content the teacher considered to be important, and what would determine the difference between high-, medium-, and low-quality essays, then this assignment would have received a higher score for this dimension.

Seventh Grade

For this assignment students read an essay and then wrote an essay summarizing the major points of the author's argument and stating whether or not they agreed with the author. Students were graded based on the accuracy of their representation of the author's argument and their ability to respond to the author's ideas. High-quality papers had more of a connection to the text than did the medium-quality papers.

As with the previous example, these criteria are quite broadly stated and would not provide much support to students seeking guidance for how to write a successful essay. The "ability to respond to the author's ideas" is not a very clear criterion. While some reference is made to the content of students' responses (e.g., the accuracy of their representation of the author's argument), not enough information is provided to students to justify a higher score for this dimension. If the criteria had been more specific with regard to what would constitute a high-quality response (e.g., articulating an opinion, or refuting or supporting specific parts of the author's argument) then this assignment would have received a higher score for this dimension.

Tenth Grade

For this assignment students answered a series of comprehension questions about a novel they had read in class. The assessment criteria for this assignment were that they end up with a "grasp of the important events in the story, complete answers with details, proper paragraph format." This assignment received a moderate score for this dimension because the grading criteria do not include much information that would help a student improve the quality of their responses. For example, it is not clear how the teacher intended to distinguish between high-, medium-, and low-quality "grasp of the important events." For this reason, this assignment also received a moderate score for this dimension.

LEVEL 3: GRADING CRITERIA ARE CLEAR AND INCLUDE A FOCUS ON ANALYSIS AND INTERPRETATION

At the next highest level of quality, the grading criteria are clearly stated with some degree of elaboration or detail. These criteria can take the form of a detailed list of dimensions upon which the work will be evaluated that do not necessarily distinguish between high-, medium-, and low-quality work. Or, the criteria can take the form of a rudimentary rubric, as opposed to a detailed list of criteria. These criteria also include a focus on having students analyze and interpret a text but do not include a focus on students' use of evidence from a text to support their responses.

Third Grade

For this assignment students wrote a retelling of a story from their basal reader. The grading criteria for this assignment were

- Accurate description of the plot, characters, setting, and main conflict in the story and how that conflict was resolved
- Accurate description of the story's theme or main idea
- Correct paragraph format (i.e., topic sentences and supporting sentences)
- Complete sentences
- Correct grammar and spelling

These criteria are clear and include a focus on students developing higher-level comprehension skills (e.g., by discussing the main theme or idea of the story, as opposed to simply reiterating the events in the story). If this list had been expanded to describe different levels of quality (e.g., the difference between good and excellent work), and if there also had been a focus on students using examples from the story to support their description of the main theme, then this assignment would have received an even higher score of 4 for this dimension.

Seventh Grade

For this assignment students wrote an evaluation of a novel. The teacher used these criteria to grade students' work:

- Introductory paragraph in which you judge the quality of the work based on a certain criteria (review your notes from our class discussions)
- At least two paragraphs where you support your judgment about the book
- Closing paragraph where your restate your judgment about the book and make a concluding statement
- Interesting word choice and vocabulary
- Correct grammar, spelling, and punctuation

- Edited first draft
- Typed final draft

These criteria describe in fairly good detail what students would need to do to receive a high score for this assignment. What the teacher expects to see included in each paragraph of the students' essays is clearly described. These criteria also include a focus on students developing complex thinking skills in the service of understanding a text (applying an external criteria to evaluate a book). As with the previous examples, this assignment received a good score for this dimension and would have received an exemplary score if the levels of quality for each of the criterion had been explicated in greater detail. For example, if the teacher had been more specific about the number or quality of the examples she expected to see in essays that received high, medium, or low scores or if she had provided more guidance with regard to the quality of the criteria students used to judge the book.

Tenth Grade

A tenth-grade assignment that illustrates a 3 for the clarity and content of the grading criteria was one in which students wrote an essay describing the main character from a novel they had read. The grading criteria for this assignment consisted of an extremely detailed list:

- Content:
    Controlling idea
    Interesting thesis
    Support for thesis
    Insight about the character
    Enough detail
- Organization:
    Five paragraphs
    Effective opening
    Smooth transitions
    Topic sentences for all paragraphs
    Sense of resolution for conclusion
- Voice and Vocabulary:
    Audience awareness

    Lively text
    Correct use of nouns and modifiers
    Interesting word choice
    Minimal repetition, clichés
  • Fluency and Writing Conventions:
    No run-sentences
    No sentence fragments
    Correct spelling and grammar
    Correct use of punctuation (including paragraph indentation)
    Final draft neatly presented and easy to read

These criteria provide good information to students about the teacher's expectations for their essays. If the criteria had specified the differences between a high-, medium-, or low-scoring essay with regard to how a student provided "insight about the character" or "enough detail," and if the criteria had included more of a focus on students' use of evidence, then this assignment would have received an even higher score of 4 for this dimension.

LEVEL 4: GRADING CRITERIA ARE VERY CLEAR AND DETAILED FOR DIFFERING LEVELS OF QUALITY STUDENT WORK AND INCLUDE A FOCUS ON ANALYSIS AND INTERPRETATION

At the highest level of quality, teachers' grading criteria generally are expressed in the form of a rubric in which each dimension is clear and explicit and varying degrees of success for each dimension are clearly articulated. Additionally, the grading criteria used to assess students' work include a focus on students analyzing and interpreting a text and using evidence from a text to support their responses (see Table 5.1).

Third Grade

    For this assignment students read a chapter book and wrote a three-paragraph essay comparing two main characters. To assess students' work, the teacher developed a four-point rubric. The criteria for obtaining the highest score on this rubric were that the student should

- Clearly address the topic
- Accurately describe the characters' qualities
- Include supporting details from the text
- Describe important similarities and differences between the characters (e.g., not just that one was short and the other was tall)
- Write at least three paragraphs, all of which should contain topic sentences
- Achieve nearly perfect spelling and punctuation

This assignment illustrates a 4 for this dimension because the rubric is extremely clear about what the teacher expects from students. The rubric also includes a focus on having students apply their analytical skills in the service of understanding the text (e.g., through discerning between more important as opposed to less important differences and similarities between the characters), as well as using evidence (details) from the story to support their writing.

Seventh Grade

For this assignment, students read a novel and wrote an essay predicting what would happen to the story's characters after the novel ended. The teacher created a five-point rubric to assess students' essays. To obtain a score of 5, the teacher used the following criteria:

- Shows a clear understanding of the situation described in the text
- Makes creative and plausible connections between causes and effects in text (i.e., teaches the reader something new)
- Uses many supporting examples

These criteria are very clear with regard to the teacher's expectations for the quality of students' work, and include a focus on students developing their analysis skills by writing about how events in the story might lead to other possible outcomes. The criteria also include a focus on students basing their predictions on the content of the novel by using many supporting examples to support their assertions (as opposed to making random or baseless speculations). For these reasons, this assignment also received the highest score for the clarity and content of the grading criteria.

Tenth Grade

A tenth-grade assignment that also received the highest score for this dimension was one in which students wrote an essay evaluating a novel. The grading criteria for this assignment—a four-point rubric with separate dimensions—was extremely detailed and focused on the quality of students' arguments (see Table 5.2).

Table 5.2   Book Evaluation Assignment Grading Criteria

	Level 4	Level 3	Level 2	Level 1
Clarity of position	Position is clear, authoritative, and defined.	Position is clear and consistent.	Position is simplistic, may be inconsistent.	Position is not clear.
Strength of argument	Argument reveals deep critical thinking.	Argument reveals complexity of thought, though there may be some gaps in logic.	Argument is superficial and/ or general.	Argument is not made, opinion may be stated with little or no rationale.
Use of evidence	Argument is supported with substantial evidence, and many details from the text are included.	Argument is supported with some evidence, and some details are included from the text.	Argument is supported by minimal evidence from the text, and few details are included from the text.	Argument is not supported by evidence.
Writing style	Essay is in proper format, transitions between paragraphs and sections are smooth, word choice is accurate and interesting, and there are almost no errors in spelling, punctuation, and grammar.	Essay is in proper format and it contains good and accurate word choices and minimal errors in spelling, punctuation, and grammar.	Essay may not follow in proper format (e.g., may lack the correct number of paragraphs), word choice is inaccurate or overly simplistic, and essay contains some errors in spelling, punctuation, and grammar.	Essay is incomplete, word choice is inaccurate or inappropriate (e.g., the use of slang), and errors in spelling, punctuation, and grammar are pervasive.

As with examples from third and seventh grades, these grading criteria are quite detailed and provide a great deal of information to students about the teacher's expectations for high-quality work. Each dimension is well articulated, and varying degrees of success are clearly defined. Additionally, these criteria include a focus on students developing strong arguments in their essays—a very complex skill—and using evidence from the novel to support their positions. For these reasons, this assignment also received the highest score for this dimension.

COMMUNICATING THE EXPECTATIONS FOR HIGH-QUALITY WORK

As described earlier in this chapter, the way in which the criteria for high-quality student work is communicated to students is as important as the quality of these criteria. Ideally, a teacher would share his or her grading criteria with students in multiple ways. For example, through class discussions, written artifacts (including posting assignment directions and criteria charts in a visible area of the classroom), and in models of high-quality work. Students also would have the opportunity to apply a teacher's grading criteria to guide and assess their own work. The purpose of this would be to support students in internalizing the standards for high-quality work, and becoming better editors and revisers of their own writing. Some ways that criteria are (or are not) shared with students are described in the following sections.

LEVEL 1: THE CRITERIA FOR HIGH-QUALITY WORK ARE NOT SHARED WITH STUDENTS IN ADVANCE OF THEIR COMPLETING THE ASSIGNMENT

At the lowest level of quality the criteria for assessing students' work is not shared with students in advance of their completing an assignment task (see Table 5.3). This could be because a teacher may not have determined her grading criteria for assessing students' work in advance of their completing an assignment. Or, a teacher may only have shared her grading criteria when she gave students their final grades. This is illustrated in the examples that follow.

Table 5.3   Communicating the Criteria for High-Quality Work to Students

Level 1	Level 2	Level 3	Level 4
Teacher does not share her criteria for assessing students' work in advance of their completing an assignment.	Teacher discusses the criteria for assessing students' work (e.g., scoring guide and rubric) with students in advance of their completing an assignment.	Teacher discusses the criteria for assessing students' work (e.g., scoring guide and rubric) with students in advance of their completing an assignment and provides students access to a written version of these criteria (e.g., a criteria chart and models of high-quality work).	Teacher discusses the criteria for assessing students' work (e.g., scoring guide and rubric) with students in advance of their completing an assignment and provides students access to a written version of these criteria. The students also are actively encouraged to apply the criteria to their own or a peer's work.

Third Grade

For this assignment, students answered a series of comprehension questions about a book they had read in class. This assignment illustrates a score of 1 for this dimension because the teacher reported that she did not have a set criteria in mind for assessing student work when she assigned the task. In her words, "I wanted to see what they could do before I decided on the criteria for grading their work." Although it is understandable that a teacher could sometimes be unsure of her expectations for high-quality work—especially if she is new to teaching, or to teaching at that grade level, or was assigning a task that was unfamiliar to students—this assignment would receive a low score for this dimension because of the lack of opportunity afforded to students to use the criteria to help shape their work. In other words, regardless of the teacher's reasons for not sharing the criteria with students in advance of their completing their work, not sharing the criteria would still diminish students' opportunity to learn. For this reason, this assignment received the lowest score for this dimension.

Seventh Grade

For this assignment, students wrote an essay comparing characters from two novels. As in the third-grade assignment, the teacher reported that she did not share her criteria with students in advance of their completing their work because, in her words, "This was a new assignment for the students, and the first time many of them have written a comparison essay. I wanted to see how they did before I decided my criteria for high-, medium-, and low-quality student work." Again, a teacher might not always have a firm idea of what she is looking for in student work if she is not experienced at giving that sort of assignment to her students. It can take a long time to develop, or accumulate from other sources, high-quality assessment tools for grading students' work. Still, the fact remains that for this assignment the students in her class did not have the opportunity to use the grading criteria as a support for shaping and structuring their work. For this reason this assignment also received a score of 1 for this dimension.

Tenth Grade

For this assignment students wrote an analytical essay about a novel they had read in class. In contrast to the examples from third and seventh grades, the teacher for this class had a rubric for grading students' work. She did not, however, share this rubric with students in *advance* of their finishing their work. Instead, students received a copy of the rubric when they received their final grades on the last draft of their essays. For this reason, this assignment also was considered to illustrate a score of 1 because students did not have the opportunity to use the rubric to help them improve their work prior to turning in the final drafts of their essays. If the teacher had discussed the rubric in class while students were working on drafts of their work, or at least provided students with a copy of the rubric to refer to when writing their essays, then this assignment would have received a higher score for this dimension.

LEVEL 2: THE CRITERIA FOR HIGH-QUALITY WORK ARE DISCUSSED IN CLASS ONLY

At the second level of quality, the criteria for high-quality student work are discussed with students in advance of their completing the assignment, but are not supported with any sort of written documentation (see Table 5.3). In other words, students have the opportunity to learn about the criteria in a class discussion but do not have access to a record of the criteria that they can refer to when completing their work.

Third Grade

For this assignment students wrote a new "chapter" (consisting of three paragraphs) for a novel they had read in class. In the teacher's words, "I explained to the students that their chapters needed to be at least three paragraphs long and that they should be consistent with the characters and events in the novel." This assignment illustrates a score of 2 for this dimension because the teacher discussed his criteria for high-quality student work—that they be three paragraphs long and consistent with the rest of the novel—but he did not provide students with a rubric or other written record of these criteria. If, for example, he had created a criteria chart with students that focused on what would constitute a good chapter and posted that chart in the classroom, or provided students with models of high-quality work that they could refer to when writing their chapters, then this assignment would have received a higher score for this dimension.

Seventh Grade

For this assignment, students answered a series of comprehension questions about a short story they had read in class. The teacher reported that "students were told in class what I was looking for in their work. For example, I wanted them to use correct paragraph format and include examples from the story when they answered the questions." Discussing with students the criteria for high-quality student work is very important. Ideally, however, students also would receive a written copy of these criteria to refer to when shaping their work. For example, rather than simply remembering to include examples from the story in their answers, ideally they would have access to written support that would guide them to consider how many examples they might need or the elements of an exemplary response. Because students did not receive this additional support, this assignment received a 2 for this dimension.

Tenth Grade

For this assignment, students wrote an evaluation of a novel they had read in class. The teacher reported that she "discussed the expectations for high-quality work with the students in class," but she did not provide them with a copy of her expectations for high-quality work. Again, as with the example from seventh grade, it is of critical importance to discuss the criteria for grading student work with students, but it is also important to provide students with access to some sort of written version of these criteria to guide students' efforts. For example, for this assignment students wrote multiple drafts of their evaluations. Having a copy of the grading criteria that clearly set forth the differences between high-, medium- and low-quality student work and that focused on the content of students' responses could have helped students when they were revising their drafts. Because students did not have this opportunity, this assignment, too, was considered to illustrate a score of 2 for this dimension.

LEVEL 3: THE CRITERIA FOR HIGH-QUALITY WORK ARE DISCUSSED IN CLASS, AND STUDENTS HAVE ACCESS TO WRITTEN FORMS OF THE CRITERIA

At the third level of quality, the teacher discusses her criteria for high-quality student work with students and provides students with access to a written record of these expectations (see Table 5.3). This written record could take multiple forms; for example, a copy of the rubric could be distributed to students, or a teacher could post her criteria for assessing student work in a public area of the classroom.

Ideally a teacher also would support these criteria with models of high-quality work that are linked to these criteria. Receiving models of high-quality work is important because it shows—in concrete form—what a teacher expects from students with regard to the quality of their work. These models can be especially powerful when they exemplify work completed by students at their same grade level. For example, an essay by Sandra Cisneros in which she writes about a character's name (from *The House on Mango Street*) could be used as a model to inspire and motivate seventh-grade students when they are assigned to write an essay on the same subject. Models of high-quality work from similarly aged students, however, might serve as a better scaffold, because they would be more proximal to students' own abilities. In other words, essays from more capable seventh graders might be a more attainable model for the rest of the class; that is, a step up rather than a giant leap.

Of course, it can be difficult to find good models of student work. It takes experience to perfect assignments and accumulate these examples. For this reason teachers could potentially support each other by sharing models of high-quality work as part of a collaborative process of developing assignments. However models are attained, or whatever models are used, it is important that students not only discuss the criteria upon which their work will be graded in class but have a concrete form of the criteria to refer to when completing their work. These issues are described in depth in the next section.

Third Grade

For this assignment students wrote an essay comparing characters from two novels. The teacher reported that she explained to her students in class the criteria she used to grade their work and that she posted these criteria in a chart at the front of the classroom. She also provided students with examples of excellent essays written by students in previous years. Because students had access in multiple forms to the teacher's expectations for high-quality work (through discussion, the posted criteria chart, and models of student work) this assignment illustrates a high score, a 3, for this dimension.

Seventh Grade

For this assignment students wrote a letter from the perspective of a novel's character. The teacher described, "I gave students a copy of the rubric I used to grade their work and reviewed the rubric with them in class before their letters were due." Because students received a copy of the rubric in advance of their completing their letters, and also reviewed these criteria with the teacher in class, this assignment was considered to illustrate a score of 3 for this dimension.

Tenth Grade

For this assignment students wrote an essay analyzing and describing the main character from a novel. The teacher reported that she provided students with a copy of the rubric that she used to grade students' work, as well as models of high-quality work from previous classes. Because students had multiple forms of access to the criteria, this assignment, too, was considered to illustrate a score of 3 for communicating to students what constituted high-quality work.

LEVEL 4: STUDENTS HAVE ACCESS TO MULTIPLE FORMS OF THE CRITERIA AND ARE ENCOURAGED TO APPLY THE CRITERIA TO THEIR OWN WORK

In addition to having access to multiple reminders of the grading criteria (e.g., in class discussions, rubrics and criteria charts, and models of high quality work), at the highest level of quality students are guided to apply these criteria to critically assess their own work (see Table 5.3). The point of this is to support students in learning how to use (and ultimately internalize or appropriate) these criteria and become more proficient at critically analyzing their own work.

Third Grade

For this assignment students wrote a report about a novel of their choice. The teacher for this assignment reported that she brainstormed with students the elements of a high-quality book report and that she posted these criteria at the front of the classroom so that students could refer to them when completing their reports. During individual conference sessions with the students she also encouraged them to refer to these criteria to help students revise their work. Because students were given access to the teacher's grading criteria in multiple ways (through a class discussion and a posted criteria chart) in advance of their completing their reports, and students were guided toward applying these criteria when revising their work, this assignment received the highest score, a 4, for this dimension.

Seventh Grade

For this assignment students wrote an evaluation of a novel they had read in class. The teacher reported that she also shared her criteria for grading students' work in multiple ways, and encouraged students to apply the rubric to evaluate their own work. Specifically, in her words, "The students and I used the rubric to grade their own essays. We then met and discussed the differences between their scores and my scores." This assignment received the highest score for this dimension because students were given access to the teacher's criteria in advance of completing their evaluations, and more importantly, were given the opportunity to apply the criteria to assess their own work. Going through this process would leave little doubt as to what the teacher considered to be high-quality work, especially since the teacher met with students individually to discuss what they had written. Applying these criteria themselves to assess their own work also provided students with a greater opportunity to develop their revision skills by internalizing the rubric.

Tenth Grade

For this assignment students wrote an essay discussing the main themes of a novel. As with the seventh-grade example, the teacher reported that she discussed her criteria for high-quality work with the students when she assigned the essay, and she provided them with a copy of her scoring rubric, as well as models of high-quality essays. Students also used this rubric to review each other's early drafts. In this teacher's words, "I wanted students to use the rubric to critique each other's work, and to help them review their work more critically." Because students had access to the criteria through class discussion, and because they received a copy of these criteria and were guided to apply them when review a peer's work, this assignment received the highest score for this dimension.

SUMMARY

The grading criteria for an assignment should clearly and explicitly communicate the standards for high-quality work to students and include a focus on meaningful, higher-level academic skills. In order for a teacher's grading criteria to fully support students' learning, however, these criteria should be shared with students in advance of their completing their work—for example, through class discussions, in some written form, and/or in grade-appropriate models of high-quality work. Ideally students also would be actively supported in their use of these criteria to shape and assess their work.

QUESTIONS TO GUIDE REFLECTION AND ANALYSIS OF THE GRADING CRITERIA USED TO ASSESS STUDENTS' WORK

1. How clear and detailed are the criteria for grading students' work?
2. Do these criteria contain enough information so that a student would understand the expectations for producing high-, medium-, and low-quality work? Do these criteria contain enough information so that students would be able to improve their work after reviewing them?
3. Do at least some of the criteria for assessing the quality of students' work focus on students analyzing and interpreting a text?
4. Do at least some of the criteria for assessing the quality of students' work focus on the quality of the evidence students use to support their answers?

QUESTIONS TO GUIDE REFLECTION AND ANALYSIS OF HOW THE GRADING CRITERIA WERE COMMUNICATED TO STUDENTS

1. Were the criteria for grading students' work discussed with them in class?
2. Did students have access to a written version of the criteria (e.g., a criteria chart posted in a visible part of the classroom, or a copy of a rubric)?
3. Did students have access to models of high-quality work that were linked to the grading criteria?
4. Were students supported to apply these criteria to analyze their own (and/or a peer's) work?

6

WRITTEN DIRECTIONS: ONE WAY TO LET STUDENTS KNOW HOW TO BE SUCCESSFUL ON AN ASSIGNMENT

The written directions for an assignment also can be an important way of conveying the expectations for high-quality work to students. In fact, researchers associated with the National Writing Project and the Educational Testing Service found that students produced higher-quality work when teachers provided them with written directions containing substantive information about how to structure and shape their work (Storms, Riazantseva, & Gentile, 2000). For example, assignments where students were prompted to describe a familiar place appeared to be more successful when the written directions guided them to consider specific sensory details (e.g., the smell, touch, or sound of a place) as well as on the amount of detail to include in their writing.

Of course, it would be inappropriate to expect very young students to read elaborate and detailed instructions for an assignment. Additionally, not every assignment given to students would necessarily include detailed written directions, especially if students completed similar assignments on a routine basis. For example, detailed assignment directions for writing a book evaluation might not be necessary at the end of the year if a teacher had provided detailed written directions to students earlier in the year and regularly reinforced these expectations in subsequent assignments. In fact, it would be desirable for students to eventually internalize a teacher's expectations for high-quality work and not need detailed directions for every assignment they completed. For tasks that are relatively unfamiliar to students, however, written directions that specify what the teacher will consider high-quality work have the potential to serve as an important source of support for student learning because, along with the grading criteria, they provide students with information they can use to guide and shape their work. The different levels of quality with regard to the clarity and content of the written assignment directions are described in the following sections.

LEVEL 1: ASSIGNMENT DIRECTIONS ARE UNCLEAR AND/OR DO NOT FOCUS ON STUDENTS' COMPREHENSION OF A TEXT

At the lowest level of quality, assignment directions are nonspecific regarding the content requirements of students' work and provide little information to students about what they need to do to successfully complete the assignment (see Table 6.1). This is most typically seen in assignment directions that focus primarily on the procedural aspects of completing an assignment, instead of on the development of the content of students' work. This is illustrated in the following examples from grades three, seven, and ten.

Table 6.1   **Providing Clear and Rigorous Written Assignment Directions**

Level 1	Level 2	Level 3
The assignment directions are nonspecific and provide little or no information to students regarding what they need to do to successfully complete the task.	The assignment directions are clear and provide general information to students regarding what they need to do, or include in their work, to successfully complete the task.	The assignment directions are clear and detailed and provide a great deal of information to students regarding what they need to do, or include in their work, to successfully complete the task.

Third Grade

The following directions for a third-grade assignment in which students answered a series of comprehension questions illustrate a score of 1 for this dimension:

"Discuss the following questions with your partner and write down your answer in the space provided. Make sure to capitalize the beginning of every sentence."

These directions let students know what they are supposed to do during class time (i.e., they are supposed to discuss the questions with their partners and write down their answers), but they provide little information to students with regard to the content of their response. Because the assignment directions given to students focused on the general steps for completing the task rather than on how to complete the task successfully, this assignment illustrates the lowest score for this dimension. If the directions had provided students with some information about what to include in their responses (e.g., how much detail or how many examples to include from the story in their answers) then this assignment would have received a higher score for this dimension.

Seventh Grade

A seventh-grade assignment that illustrates the lowest score, a 1, for this dimension was one in which students wrote a response to an essay they had read in a popular news magazine. The directions provided to students for this assignment were to "Write a response to the article we read in class. Make sure to write at least two paragraphs and explain your thoughts."

These written directions, although more informative than the directions for the third-grade example, do not provide a great deal of direction to students with regard to what the teacher was looking for in the students' work. While it is clear that the teacher wants students to produce at least two paragraphs and explain their thoughts, what she means by wanting the students to respond to the article is not as clear. For example, did she want students to state whether or not they agreed with the actions described in the article? Did she want them to write their thoughts about the topic in general? What sort of evidence was she looking for to determine whether students had explained their thoughts adequately? Because the directions given to the students (in written form at least) were unclear with regard to the content of the students' responses, this assignment received a low score for the clarity and content of the written directions.

Tenth Grade

The directions for the tenth-grade assignment also illustrate a score of 1 for this dimension. For this assignment students wrote a description of a character from *I Know Why the Caged Bird Sings* by Maya Angelou. The assignment directions were as follows:

> Write at least three paragraphs describing one of the characters from *I Know Why the Caged Bird Sings*. Remember to follow correct paragraph format (topic sentence, supporting sentences, and concluding sentence).

These written assignment directions are again quite general with regard to what students needed to do or include in their essays to successfully complete the task. For example, were students supposed to describe the character's physical appearance and role in the story? Were they supposed to describe the character's general personality characteristics or relationships with other people? The type of detail students were to include from the text also was not explained. For example, did the teacher want the students to support their descriptions with quotes or other text-specific references? Because the written directions provided to students were unclear and did not focus on supporting the development of higher-level content in students' work, this assignment received the lowest score for the clarity and content of the assignment directions.

LEVEL 2: WRITTEN DIRECTIONS ARE BROADLY STATED AND/OR FOCUS ON STUDENTS' ATTAINMENT OF A SURFACE-LEVEL UNDERSTANDING OF A TEXT

At the second level of quality, the assignment directions provided to students are clear but broadly stated and provide only a general description of what students are to include in their written work. These directions touch on the content of students' work, but they do not support students in applying higher-level thinking skills in the service of deeply understanding a text (see Table 6.1).

Third Grade

A score of 2 for this dimension is illustrated in directions for a third-grade assignment in which students summarized a chapter from *Beezus and Ramona* by Beverly Cleary. These directions were as follows:

Beezus and Ramona

You will summarize chapter five ("A Party at the Quimbys"). Make sure that your summary includes a description of the problem in the chapter and how that problem was solved. Remember also to write in proper paragraph form and use correct spelling and punctuation. Your summary should be at least one page long, and you can include an illustration if you want.

These directions provide only minimal information to students regarding what they would need to include in their summary to successfully complete the task (i.e., describing the problem in the chapter and the solution to the problem). Additionally, these directions do not guide students to analyze the chapter beyond identifying the problem (i.e., that Ramona invites her friends over for a party without informing her mother) and the solution to that problem (i.e., that Beezus leads the children in a parade and her mother feeds the children leftover applesauce). If the directions had prompted students to write about the main themes in the book (e.g., the differences in Beezus' and Ramona's characters and how that influenced their relationship, the ups and downs of having a sibling, whether or not siblings always love each other, and what Beezus and Ramona potentially teach each other) and to connect these ideas to the events in this chapter, then these directions likely would have received a higher score for this dimension.

Seventh Grade

For this assignment students wrote a report about a book of their choice. The directions for this assignment were as follows:

Directions for Writing Book Reports

1. Introduction (1 paragraph):

    In the introduction you should briefly describe the book and finish the paragraph by stating *what you think about it*. This is your thesis statement, or main idea or position you are arguing.

2. Reason 1 (1 paragraph):

    In the body of your essay you should state what you think and why. *You should have one reason for each paragraph* and you should use examples from the book to support your reasons.

3. Reason 2 (1 paragraph)

    See #2

4. Reason 2 (1 paragraph)

    See #2

5. Conclusion (1 paragraph)

    In the conclusion, restate your introduction, but turn it around. First, restate your thesis (or main idea or position you are arguing) using different words. Then summarize your reasons in 2–3 sentences. End your report with an interesting comment, a question, or a recommendation.

These directions are clear, but they are quite generic with regard to essay writing. In other words, they provide little guidance about the issues students should address in the content of their book reports and instead focus more on the format of students' responses. If students had been guided to focus more on the content of their reports in these directions—for example, by identifying the book's main themes or ideas or applying an external criteria for evaluating the book—then this assignment likely would have received a higher score for this dimension.

Tenth Grade

A tenth-grade assignment that also illustrates a score of 2 for the clarity and content of the assignment directions was one in which students read *1984* by George Orwell and wrote an essay comparing the society portrayed in that book with contemporary U.S. society. The teacher's written directions to the students for this essay were as follows:

1984 Essay

In a well-developed essay compare and contrast the society portrayed in *1984* with our society today. Include in your discussion the balance between conformity and individualism. Your essay should be at least five paragraphs long and should include specific examples from the novel to support your argument.

These directions are clear with regard to the general issues students are to address in their essays, but they provide little assistance to students on how to go about addressing these issues in their essays. If these directions had provided more information to students with regard to how to structure their essays and approach these issues, this assignment would have received a higher score for this dimension.

LEVEL 3: WRITTEN DIRECTIONS ARE CLEAR AND INCLUDE A FOCUS ON ANALYSIS AND INTERPRETATION

At the highest level of quality, the written assignment directions are clear and detailed and provide a great deal of information to students about what they would need to do to meet the teacher's expectations for the content of their work. The directions also provide students with guidance on how to analyze and interpret what they read (see Table 6.1).

Third Grade

A score of 3 is illustrated in the following assignment from a third-grade classroom. For this assignment students summarized *The Big Wave* by Pearl Buck. These were the written directions provided to students:

Book Report for *The Big Wave*

Your book report should be at least two pages long and should include lots of details from the story. Please remember to describe:

- The author and title of the book
- What the story was about (the plot)
- Where the story took place (the setting)

- Who the main characters were
- The main theme of the story (what we talked about in class)
- The main conflict in the story
- How the conflict was resolved

Please remember to follow proper paragraph format in your reports.

These directions were fairly informative with regard to the expected length of students' responses and the issues the teacher wanted students to address in their reports to obtain a good grade. The directions also guide students to consider the main theme of the story and reminds students to think about what they had talked about in class, in addition to writing about the main conflict in the story and how the conflict was resolved. For these reasons, this assignment received a high score for the clarity and content of the assignment directions.

Seventh Grade

An assignment that also illustrates a 3 for this dimension is one in which students wrote a report based on the book *Slake's Limbo* by Felice Holman. The written assignment directions provided to students for this report were as follows:

Book Report for *Slake's Limbo*

For this assignment you will write a book report analyzing and critiquing the plot of *Slake's Limbo* by Felice Holman. Your essay should be at least five paragraphs long. You also will be graded on your use of proper paragraph format, spelling, and punctuation. Your essay should include the following:

1. Introduction (1 paragraph)

- Name of novel (Slake's Limbo), author (Felice Holman)
- A few sentences describing the book
- Your opinion regarding the author's effectiveness at developing the plot

2. Plausibility of the Novel's Plot (1–2 paragraphs)

- Is the plot plausible? Give examples from the book of events that you think are plausible and/or unrealistic. How does this contribute to keeping the reader interested?

3. High Point of the Novel (Climax) (1–2 paragraphs)

- Describe the high point in the novel. Is it a climax or an anticlimax? Explain your answer. Was there any foreshadowing? If so, give an example.

4. Conclusion of the Novel (1–2 paragraphs)

- Was the conclusion adequate? Did you feel a sense of completeness? Did the author leave the reader hanging? If so, why might she have done this?

5. Conclusion (1 paragraph)

- Summarize basic points of your analysis and finish by stating again (using different words) how well you believe the author developed the plot in the novel.

These directions focus a great deal on the content of students' responses; for example, they guide students to consider the plausibility of the story and to write about the nature of the story's conclusion (i.e., why the author left the conclusion open ended). The directions also provide a great deal of information to students regrding what issues to address in their essays in order to receive high scores on their reports. For these reasons, these directions received the highest score, a 3, for this dimension.

Tenth Grade

An assignment that also received the highest score for this dimension was one in which students wrote an analytical essay about a novel they had read in class. The teacher's written directions for this assignment were as follows:

Please follow the following guidelines when writing your essays. Your essay must be at least five pages and should follow the format described below. Also remember it that should include specific examples from the text, with page numbers.

1. Introduction (1–2 paragraphs)

- Background information about the book (author, title, when written, fiction or non-fiction)
- General description of what book was about

2. Analysis of the Setting (2–3 paragraphs)

- Where does most of the action in the story happen?
- How does this influence the action in the story?

3. Analysis of the plot (2–3 paragraphs)

- What is the book about?
- What are the most important events in the book that move the plot along?
- What is the climax of the book?

4. Analysis of the Characters (2–3 paragraphs)

- Who is the protagonist? Who is the antagonist?
- What kinds of conflicts do the characters face? How do they overcome their problems?
- Do they change a lot over the course of the story (i.e., are they dynamic?) or do they stay the same (i.e., are they static?)?
- Do you learn a lot about them, or do you know only a few things? Do they feel like real people, or are they "flat?"

5. Analysis of the Themes (2–3 paragraphs)

- What are the most important themes in the book (e.g., freedom, forgiveness, love, friendship, etc.)?
- What is the author's message in the story (i.e., what was she trying to convey by writing the book)?
- How do the developments in the plot or characters contribute to the theme of the book?

6. Conclusion (1–2 paragraphs)

- Restatement of general points from your analysis
- Is this book relevant to the world today?

These assignment directions are extremely detailed and provide a great deal of information to students regarding what they should include and address in the content of their essays. While they are not specific to the book students read in class, these insightful, reflective questions still guide students in their analysis of the text. Because of the specificity and clarity of these assignment directions and their potential for supporting the development of students' analytical skills, this assignment received the highest score, a 3, for the clarity and content of the written directions.

SUMMARY

Assignment directions have the potential to support student performance when they provide information about what students should include in their work to obtain a high grade and when they support students in developing their skills at analyzing and interpreting a text. Of course, it may not always be necessary to provide students with detailed directions for all assignments, especially if it is clear that students have already internalized a teacher's expectations for high-quality work. Providing students with a written form of the expectations for an assignment task— especially for a task that is relatively unfamiliar or challenging to students—that they can refer to when producing their work, however, can be a powerful tool for supporting student performance

QUESTIONS TO GUIDE REFLECTION AND ANALYSIS OF THE WRITTEN ASSIGNMENT DIRECTIONS PROVIDED TO STUDENTS

1. Do the assignment directions provide enough guidance to students with regard to what they would need to do, or include in their work, to be successful on this assignment?
2. Do the directions include a focus on students analyzing and interpreting a text?
3. Do the directions include a focus on the quality of the evidence students use to support their answers?

7

FEEDBACK THAT IMPROVES THINKING AND WRITING

As described in Chapter 5, classroom assessment tools ideally serve a formative function by providing students with information about how to improve their written work. This is one reason why students need clear and rigorous grading criteria that provide them with information about what they need to do to succeed at a specific task. Moreover, they need to have access to assessment criteria in advance of their completing an assignment, or while they are completing an assignment, so that they have an opportunity to apply these criteria to improve their work.

Another, perhaps even more powerful, opportunity for providing formative feedback to students, however, is to write comments on drafts of their written work. The process approach to writing instruction—where students draft, edit, revise, and redraft their work over several iterations—is the standard for instruction in many school districts and states. In this approach, feedback from teachers and/or peers and the opportunity to revise written work based on this feedback are key to students' development as thinkers and writers. Providing feedback on early drafts of students' compositions creates an opportunity for teachers to give students instruction that is more explicit and individualized than a grade or a rubric score.

Although feedback on drafts of student work could provide students with the means to substantively improve their written work, research in classrooms indicates that the potential of the process approach to writing is not always realized in practice (Applebee, 1984; Matsumura, Patthey-Chavez, Valdés, & Garnier, 2002; Patthey-Chavez, Matsumura, & Valdés, 2004). Both my research and the research of others indicates, for example, that students often do not receive feedback that supports the improvement of the content of their writing. Student work very often shows improvement in grammar, punctuation, and spelling from first to final draft but remains virtually unchanged in terms of content. When students do receive content-focused feedback on early drafts of their work, however, the quality of their work improves.

As every teacher who has faced a mountain of essays to grade knows, providing individual feedback on drafts of students' essays is very hard and time-consuming work. Because individual feedback is so important for improving student writing, and so effortful for teachers, it is important that students receive the type of feedback that will most improve the content of their writing. It also is important to follow up with students to ensure that they incorporate this feedback into their subsequent drafts. For example, students could return their previous draft along with their newest draft (so that a teacher could see what he or she had written previously and how the student had revised based on that feedback). Or, for older students, a teacher could ask students to write a letter explaining how they revised their work based on the feedback they received earlier. However a teacher chooses to follow through, it is important that students be held responsible for incorporating the feedback they receive in their revisions.

The bottom line is that the time a teacher takes to provide feedback should be used to the greatest effect. This chapter describes what this feedback would look like in practice; that is, when to give comments on students' papers, and how to give feedback that pushes students to clarify their ideas, sharpen their thinking, and support their ideas and claims with examples from a text.

LEVEL 1: FEEDBACK DOES NOT SUPPORT STUDENT REVISION

At the first level of quality, students do not have the opportunity to use teacher comments to revise their work (see Table 7.1). This could be because a teacher did not provide any comments on drafts of a student's work. Alternatively, some teachers seem to reserve their most substantive written feedback for the final drafts of students' writing. This could be considered a lost opportunity for student learning for the following reasons: First, it is not clear whether or not students actually attend to the written comments on their final drafts. It is possible that students may be more concerned with their final grade or rubric score (the end product of summative assessment), than they are with teacher commentary. Additionally, and more importantly perhaps, it is not clear whether or not students apply the lessons learned from the comments on the final drafts of their papers to their next assignment. Students, therefore, may not learn as much from these final comments as they would if they had received similar information earlier and could use this information as a guide for revising their work. This is illustrated in the following examples.

Third Grade

For this third-grade assignment students wrote a new final chapter to the book *Mr. Popper's Penguins* by Richard and Florence Atwater. One student's final paper, considered by the teacher to be of medium quality for the class, consisted of very short paragraphs (one to two sentences

Table 7.1   Providing Content-Specific Feedback on Drafts of Students' Work

Level 1	Level 2	Level 3
Students did not receive comments on early drafts of their compositions. There was little or no guidance for revision.	Students received comments on early drafts of their compositions that focused on surface-level features of their writing (grammar, punctuation, spelling, and language use). Guidance for revision focused on improving the mechanics of students' writing.	Students received comments on early drafts of their compositions that focused on content of their writing (as well as surface-level features). Guidance for revision focused on improving the content of students' compositions, as well as the mechanics of their writing.

long). The teacher's comment on the final draft of this student's paper was, "Please remember that a paragraph contains a topic sentence, 2–3 supporting sentences and (usually) a closing sentence." This is important information that the student could have conceivably used to reorganize (and improve) her writing. While it is possible that this student might remember the teacher's comment and apply it to her next paper, she likely would have benefited more by revising her current paper and adding supporting and concluding sentences to her paragraphs. For this reason, this assignment received the lowest score, a 1, with regard to students' opportunity to revise their work based on teachers' written comments.

Seventh Grade

For this assignment students wrote evaluations of a novel. On one student paper, considered by the teacher to be of medium quality for the class, the teacher provided almost no written feedback on the early drafts of a student's paper. On the final draft of this student's paper, the teacher wrote, "Well organized. Could have used more specific details, quotes, and anecdotes from the book to support your statements." As with the third-grade example, this is very important feedback that would have improved the quality of the student's essay had he been given the chance to apply this instructional point in his revision and to add more details and examples from the book to support his claims.

Tenth Grade

For this assignment students read diaries of teenagers living in the nineteenth century and wrote an essay comparing their lives to the lives of these teenagers. As with the previous example, the teacher wrote almost no comments on the first draft. On the final draft, however, the teacher wrote extensive comments about the style and content of each student's paper. Specifically, she noted places where students needed to strengthen their arguments and support their statements with more examples from the texts. For example, she wrote comments such as, "Needs a clear introduction with who, what, where, and a focusing thesis: What is the essay about?" and "What are your opinions (supported by evidence) about the differences between life then and life now?" She also noted places in the essays where students needed to better organize their ideas. For example, she wrote comments such as, "You're moving from an introduction into details that belong in the body of the essay," and, "Needs topic sentence. What is your point here?" These are insightful comments that have a lot of potential for supporting significant revision on the part of the students. Unfortunately, as with the third- and seventh-grade essays described above, the students did not have the chance to use the teacher's excellent feedback to improve their work because they only received this feedback on their final drafts. For this reason, this assignment also received the lowest score for students' opportunity to revise their work based on teachers' written comments.

Of course summative comments can be instructive for students, especially when they provide students with an explanation for why they received a specific grade. For example, a third-grade teacher wrote the following comment on a student paper she considered to be of high quality, "Well done! Your chapter is adventurous. It also has a clear beginning, middle and end." This is an example of constructive positive feedback because the teacher told the student exactly why she liked the story (as opposed to simply writing, "Well done!" or "Good job!"). The point is not that summative comments are useless but that comments provided to students on early drafts can be used to improve the quality of students' writing.

LEVEL 2: FEEDBACK SUPPORTS SURFACE-LEVEL STUDENT REVISION

At the second level of quality, comments on early drafts of students' papers focus solely on improving the surface-level features of their writing— that is grammar, spelling, punctuation, and language use (see Table 7.1). This is illustrated in the examples of student essays that follow.

Third Grade

After reading a story about a fruit and vegetable seller, students wrote a short composition describing the type of store they would like to own, Excerpts from the first and final drafts of this story are included here.

First Draft

If I wloud have my own store. It would be a jewelery store. It would be called "Jewelery of the Universe!!" It would have every single jewel. It would be on Lincoln blvd. My biggest diamond would be $2,000 and my smallest would cost $200.

I would have some of my friends and family members work at the store. There will be 5 registers in the store. I will work at one of them. My mom will be the boss of the store. My sister and brother will be the other registers. We will have a lot of money and will have fun.

Final Draft

If I would have my own store. It would be a jewelry store. It would be called "Jewelry of the World!" It would have every single jewel. It would be on Lincoln Blvd. My biggest diamond would cost $2,000 and my smallest would cost $200.

I would have some of my friends and family members work at the store. There would be five registers in the store. I will work at one of them. My mom will be the boss of the store. My sister and brother will be at the other register. We will have a lot of money and we will have fun.

The teacher made numerous edits on the first draft of this student's essay. For example, "wloud" was changed to "would," "would be $2000" was changed to "would cost $2000," and "5" was changed to "five," and these (and numerous other similar edits) were reflected on the final draft. This assignment received a 2 for this dimension, however, because students were not given any direction for revising their work aside from improving the mechanics of their writing. For example, students were not asked to add or delete information or provide additional detail to expand on what they had written. The end result was a final draft that showed some improvement in terms of writing conventions but was virtually identical with regard to content.

Seventh Grade

For this assignment students wrote an essay about the heroic qualities of a character from *Flowers for Algernon* by Daniel Keyes. Excerpts from a student's essay are shown here.

First Draft

"Flowers for Algernon" is about a man named Charlie who has a learning disorder. He goes through a lot of difficulties in his life and will do almost anything to improve his IQ. Charlie does this by being an experiment for a surgery. I think that he was extremely brave for doing this because who knows how the surgery would turn out . . .

   At the end of the story the results of surgery faded away and Charlie went back to his normal IQ. He made a very big desision [*sic*]; it was to go live on his own. I felt that Charlie was very brave for this because now he can be and feel independent and not expect other people to do things for him.

Final Draft

"Flowers for Algernon" is about a man named Charlie who has a learning disorder. He goes through a lot of difficulties in his life and will do almost anything to improve his IQ. Charlie does this by going through experimental surgery. I think he was extremely brave for doing this because no one knew how the surgery would turn out . . .

   At the end of the story the results of surgery faded away and Charlie went back to his normal IQ. He made a very big decision. It was to go live on his own. I felt that Charlie was very brave for this because now he can be and feel independent and not expect other people to do things for him.

As shown above, the teacher made some changes to the initial draft. Notably, "Charlie does this by being an experiment for a surgery" was changed to "Charlie does this by going through experimental surgery." Additionally "knows" was changed to "knew" at the end of the first paragraph, and one spelling error was corrected ("decision"). Beyond that, however, the two drafts were virtually identical. For the final paragraph especially, there is certainly room for the student to expand on why the character (Charlie) was brave for deciding to live on his own. The student did not receive this type of guidance for revising his essay, however, and did not do so on his own.

Tenth Grade

   The following assignment illustrates a score of 2 for the guidance students received to revise their essays. For this assignment students wrote an essay about the play *The Crucible* by Arthur Miller. Excerpts from drafts of a student's essay are shown here.

First Draft

In the crucible fanaticism is a very important theme. By the end of act three 72 people total are convicted of witchery. Fanaticism is very influential in these convictions because it was like an addiction. Many people are falsely accused of being witches and are hung. Rumors that women are practicing witchcraft galvanize the town's most basic fears and suspicions. When Abigail accuses Elizabeth Procter of being a witch Church and townspeople insist on taking Elizabeth on trial.

Final Draft

In "The Crucible" fanaticism is a very important theme. By the end of act three 72 people total are convicted of witchery. Fanaticism is very influential in these convictions because it was like an addiction. Many people are falsely accused of being witches and are hung. Rumors that women are practicing witchcraft encourage the town's most basic fears and suspicions. For example, when Abigail accuses Elizabeth Procter of being a witch the Church and townspeople insist on taking Elizabeth to trial.

As shown above, the drafts of these essays are virtually identical, albeit with corrected grammar and some changes in language use. For example, the teacher had the student change "galvanize" to "encourage," "taking Elizabeth on trial" was changed to "taking Elizabeth to trial," and "for example" was added in the second to the last sentence. What is notable, however, is how similar the drafts were from first to final form. The teacher did not seize on opportunities to have the student expand and support broad statements. The content of the essay would have been improved, for example, if the statement "Fanaticism is very influential in these convictions because it was like an addiction" had been expanded on and supported with examples from the play when the student revised his final draft. Because the teacher's written comments focused solely on students improving the surface-level features of their writing, this assignment received a 2 for student's opportunity to use a teacher's written comments to revise their work.

LEVEL 3: FEEDBACK SUPPORTS CONTENT-LEVEL STUDENT REVISION

In general, feedback that directly addresses what the student has written and contains specific suggestions for revision appears to be more helpful to students then general remarks such as "needs work" or "good job" (see Table 7.1). Examples of comments that challenge students' thinking and help them revise the contents of their drafts include asking students to expand on their statements, explain their ideas, think more deeply about a text, correct errors in understanding, and connect their statements to a main idea or thesis (i.e., develop an argument). In addition to challenging students' thinking and helping them develop their ideas, teacher feedback also can improve the content of students' writing by guiding them to use evidence from the text to support their ideas at key points in their writing. Examples of these types of content-specific feedback are presented in the following examples from third, seventh, and tenth grades.

Third Grade

For this assignment, which received the highest score for this dimension, students wrote descriptions of a character from *Tales of a Fourth-Grade Nothing* by Judy Blume. The following are drafts of a student's composition for this assignment.

First Draft

Fudge is Peter's little brother. Fudge was being nosy. He wrote all over Peter's poster. Fudge was a spoiled baby because he's [*sic*] mother loves him more than Peter. When Fudge wrote all over Peter's paper she spank [*sic*] him.

Final Draft

Fudge is Peter's little brother. Fudge was being nosy. He wrote all over Peter's poster. Fudge was a spoiled baby because he's [*sic*] mother loves him more than Peter. When Fudge wrote all over Peter's paper she spank [*sic*] him.

Fudge's personality is he's hyper. For example, he went on the monkey bars and flapped his wings like a bird and then he fell and broke his front teeth. Fudge always follow Peter and bothers him.

At the end of the first draft, the teacher wrote, "Write another paragraph and tell me more about Fudge. Use examples from the story to describe what Fudge is like." As shown in this example, while imperfect, the content of the student's essay shows definite improvement from the first to second draft. Notably, the student heeded the teacher's comments and added a new paragraph that contained more information about Fudge's character. The student also included an example from the text illustrating how he had a "hyper" personality (i.e., "he went on the monkey bars and flapped his wings like a bird . . . ").

Seventh Grade

For this assignment the content of the students' writing also was improved through the teacher's suggestion that more examples be added to the text. For this assignment students wrote essays summarizing the book *Treasure Island* by Robert Louis Stevenson. Excerpts from the first and final drafts of a student's essay are included here.

First Draft

This story is interesting because when you read it is like so different parts of the story make it exciting. I mean it is always fun to read a story about treasure. There were a lot of exciting parts in the story. Such as parts like when the bad side almost tries to kill the good side. It is interesting because it gets you anxious to know what happens.

Final Draft

This story is interesting because when you read it is like so different parts of the story make it exciting. I mean it is always fun to read a story about treasure. There were a lot of exciting parts in the story. Such as parts like when the bad people tries to kill the good. It is interesting because it gets you anxious to know what happens next. Like when Ben goes in the barrel to get some apples and hears the conversation of Long John and Dick.

It was exciting when Dick was going to get an apple for Long John but Israel Hands changed the subject to drinking rum. Or another part was when Ben and his mother get Flint's papers from the captain's chest and escaped from Pew and his crew. That was scary cause they could have caught them and get rid of them "for good."

At the end of this paragraph in the first draft the teacher wrote, "You need to add some examples from the book here." As shown in the final draft, the student heeded the teacher's comments and added two examples describing specific events in the story that were exciting ("Like when Ben goes in the barrel to get some apples and hears the conversation of Long John and Dick. It was exciting when Dick was going to get an apple for Long John but Israel Hands changed the subject to drinking rum. Or another part was when Ben and his mother get Flint's papers from the captain's chest and escaped from Pew and his crew.") The end result was a final essay that was still problematic in terms of syntax but included more evidence from the story to support the student's claims. Additional support for revising both the language and expanding on the examples given by the student likely would have improved the quality of the student's work even more.

Tenth Grade

The following assignment also illustrates a score of 3 for students' opportunity to revise their work based on a teacher's written comments. For this assignment students analyzed the poem "Alone" by Maya Angelou. Students wrote a first draft and then revised their drafts based on the teacher's edits and comments. Specifically, the teacher on the first draft of one student's essay asked the student to expand on his closing statement. On his first draft the student wrote, "I do agree with her that everyone need companionship, money can't buy your soul a home (stanza three) and the race of man will come to a terrible end if there isn't love (stanza five)." At the end of this statement the teacher wrote, "Restate this last sentence as a separate concluding paragraph. What does the author want us to do? How does she think the race of man could be saved?" The student then wrote a new concluding paragraph:

It is my opinion that Angelou wants people to be in harmony with each other. To do this she thinks that we should form a close relationship with God. If you don't believe in God then you could at least be close with another person. I agree with her and also believe that if everyone tries to do this, someday this goal will be achieved and the world will be better for everyone.

Through being prompted by the teacher to think about the author's desire for the reader, the student's second draft showed a deeper understanding of the poem's message. The feedback thus appeared to push the student to think more about the content of the poem, and this was reflected in the expanded content.

SUMMARY

Comments teachers make on student papers can play a significant part in helping students improve the content of their writing. If these comments are to help students revise their essays, however, it is important that they receive the most substantive comments on early drafts of their writing. Students should be encouraged (and even held accountable) for incorporating this feedback in their final drafts. Additionally, it is important that students receive comments that contain specific suggestions for improving the content of their writing. Edits that focus on the surface-level features of a student's work (e.g., grammar, punctuation, spelling, and word usage) will not lead to improvements in the content of students' writing and will not guide them to having a deeper understanding of the subject at hand. Types of comments that do appear to lead to improvement in the content of student's essays include asking students to expand on their statements, explain and clarify their ideas, correct errors in understanding, and support their claims with text-based evidence.

QUESTIONS TO GUIDE REFLECTION AND ANALYSIS OF THE QUALITY OF THE FEEDBACK PROVIDED TO STUDENTS ON DRAFTS OF THEIR WORK

1. Did students receive feedback on the content of their writing on early drafts of their compositions (and so have the opportunity to incorporate these comments in their revisions)?

2. If the assignment required students to produce multiple drafts of their written work, did students receive written comments that focused on the content of their writing in addition to corrections in their grammar, spelling, punctuation, and language use?

3. Did students incorporate the feedback they received on early drafts of their writing in their later drafts?

8

ARE STUDENTS LEARNING WHAT WAS INTENDED? ALIGNING THE ASSIGNMENT TASK WITH THE LEARNING GOALS

The final steps in developing an assignment involve looking back at the learning goals and checking to see that these are realized in the assignment task and in the grading criteria. As described in Chapters 3 and 4, goals for student learning ideally are clear and specific and focused at least in part on the attainment of complex thinking skills or academically rigorous content. Regardless of the quality of the learning goals, however, student learning will not be furthered if these are not aligned with the assignment activity. For example, a task for which a teacher holds the development of higher-level skills as her goal for student learning will not accomplish this goal if all students actually are required to do is recall basic facts.

Research indicates that aligning assignment activities with goals for student learning can be challenging for many teachers (Clare & Aschbacher, 2001; Matsumura, Garnier, Pascal, & Valdés, 2002), and so this chapter provides support for achieving this. As a general rule, however, it appears that a mismatch between a teacher's learning goals and an assignment task is less likely to occur when the learning goals emphasize basic skills. In other words, a teacher whose learning goal is that students recall basic facts about a story generally will create an assignment task that guides students to answer straightforward information about a story. The actual problem of mismatch between learning goals and the assignment task seems to occur more commonly when teachers hold higher-level skills as goals for student learning. This is not surprising, given that there is little consensus about what it means to analyze, interpret, or evaluate a text (terms that are frequently used in state and district standards for English language arts).

Additionally, as described earlier, teachers can hold learning goals that are quite general. This poses an additional barrier to creating assignment tasks that further specific learning aims. Just about any activity, for example, could be considered to fit a goal that is as general as "learning reading comprehension" or "developing writing skills." The clearer and more specific a teacher's goals are for student learning, the more precisely he or she would be able to create lesson activities that further these learning goals. This dimension—the alignment of the goals for student learning and the assignment task—considers, therefore, the clarity and specificity of the teacher's goals as well as the match between these goals and the structure of the assignment task. To receive the highest score on this dimension the learning goals would be very clear and specific and these goals would be fully realized in the design of the assignment task. In other words, what students were asked to do would overlap completely with the teacher's goals for student learning. Examples illustrating the different degrees of alignment between learning goals and assignment tasks are presented in the sections that follow.

LEVEL 1: GOALS FOR STUDENT LEARNING ARE NOT ALIGNED WITH THE ASSIGNMENT TASK

At the lowest level of quality for this dimension, there is a clear mismatch between a teacher's goals for student learning and the structure of the assignment task given to students (see Table 8.1). What the teacher intends for students to learn is not reflected in what students are actually asked to do. This is illustrated in a third-grade assignment in which students read *Clean Your Room, Harvey Moon!* by Pat Cummings (a below-grade-level text) and answered a series of comprehension questions. The teacher's goals for this assignment were "to develop higher-level thinking skills using questions from Bloom's taxonomy."

While the teacher refers to the development of deeper-level thinking skills as a goal for this assignment, the questions that were asked of students primarily focused on the recall of basic information from the text—a lower-level thinking skill. Additionally, students were not asked to explain their reasoning, or provide any sort of extended response. In fact, they were given very little room (two lines) to write their answers. The nature and structure of the assignment task, therefore, did not appear to match the teacher's desired goals of developing more complex thinking skills on the part of the students. The following is an excerpt of student work for this assignment:

Clean Your Room, Harvey Moon!

Why didn't Harvey want to clean his room? Because his room was a mess.

What kinds of things did Harvey find in his room? Two towels and swim trunks. Under the dresser was a gray lump that he didn't recognize and marbles and crayons and flat bottle caps.

What did Harvey do with all the stuff he found while he cleaned his room? He was put it under the rug.

Why do you think Harvey did this? Because his mom told him.

What did Harvey's mom think about the way he cleaned his room? Not really amazed.

Table 8.1   Aligning the Goals for Student Learning With the Assignment Task

Level 1	Level 2	Level 3
The learning goals and the assignment task are not aligned.	The learning goals and the assignment task are partially aligned or are aligned at a very general level.	The learning goals and the assignment task are fully aligned. Goals are clear and specific, and these goals are furthered through the lesson activity.

Seventh Grade

A seventh-grade assignment that illustrates the lowest score for this dimension was one in which students read the novel *The Witch of Blackbird Pond* by Elizabeth George Speare and completed a literature log. The teacher's goals for this assignment were that students "write responses to literature through interpreting, connecting, questioning, predicting, and evaluating." An examination of the student work for this assignment, however, revealed that students wrote only short summaries of each of the chapters. Because there was no evidence in the student work that students had been guided to interpret, connect, question, predict, or evaluate the story, this assignment was considered to exhibit a poor match between the teacher's learning goals and assignment task. The following is an excerpt from a student's literature log:

The Witch of Blackbird Pond Literature Log

Chapter 1—There was a boy named Nathaniel Eaton who was traveling with his family. He starts to meet people on the ship. The child lost her doll and she started acting crazy. It was a new doll so she was very mad, but her mother was yelling at her. The mother told the captain to turn back, but he would not listen.

Chapter 2—Kit became miserable because of the child Prudence. This child ate the tiny portions that the mother had on her plate. She couldn't get Prudence out of her mind. Kit came upon the girl and the girl looked very sad and afraid. Her mother made a harsh call and the girl went running.

Chapter 3—Kit came across a man with a leather coat and breeches. He stared at her pretty shoes. Kit finally got to meet her cousins Judith and Mercy. They had a wonderful time talking because they had never seen each other before and it was nice to catch up on things.

Tenth Grade

A tenth-grade assignment that illustrates a score of 1 for this dimension was one in which students read *I Know Why the Caged Bird Sings* by Maya Angelou and wrote an essay about freedom. The teacher's goals for this assignment were that students "connect the themes of the book to their own experience of freedom." The actual assignment task, however, only required students to write about what freedom meant to them personally, an essay they could have written without reading the book. Students were not guided to engage directly with the theme of freedom as it manifested itself in the book or to explicitly connect this to their own lives. The following is an excerpt from a student's essay:

"What Freedom Means to Me"

Being free means that you have rights. It does not mean doing what you want whenever you want to. Being free is being able to express yourself without anyone telling you what to say, and being friends with whoever you want to. It also means that you have the right to live wherever you want to without anyone or the government telling you that you cannot live there.

LEVEL 2: GOALS FOR STUDENT LEARNING ARE PARTIALLY ALIGNED WITH THE ASSIGNMENT TASK

At the second level of quality, a teacher's learning goals and the assignment task are partially aligned or are aligned at a very general level (see Table 8.1). As described earlier, teachers sometimes hold goals for student learning that are quite broad and nonspecific. When this is the case, the assignment task can match the learning goals, but the relationship between the two may not be very precise. This is exemplified in the following assignment from a third-grade classroom.

Third Grade

For this assignment students wrote a retelling of the story *My Great-Aunt Arizona* by Gloria Houston. The teacher's learning goals for this assignment were "reading comprehension and writing skills." As with the previous example, the task (basically, summarizing the story) and the learning goals were aligned, but at a very general level. Many different assignment tasks could "match" the goal of "reading comprehension," and these goals tell us very little about what the teacher intended for students to learn as a result of completing the assignment. For this reason, this assignment received a 2 for this dimension. The following is an example of student work considered by the teacher to be of medium quality for the class:

My Great Aunt Arizona

Arizona lived in a cabin that her father built. She loved to read books. When it snowed her brother and her made snow cream to eat. When it was spring, they would make a hole in the tree and put a bucket. The sap that come out it tasted like sugar. Then one day her mother died and they were very sad. Then her father went to look for a wife. When growed [*sic*] up she was a teacher. She got married with a carpenter and had a baby. Arizona lived to the age of 93.

Seventh Grade

A teacher's learning goals for an assignment also could be considered to be somewhat aligned with the assignment task if they were only partially aligned, in other words, if only some of the learning goals were realized in the assignment task. This is illustrated in the following assignment based on a play version of *A Christmas Carol* by Charles Dickens. In this example, seventh-grade students were asked to list the personality traits of the character Scrooge at the beginning and end of the story. The teacher's goals for this assignment were that students "learn to describe dynamic characters by pulling out characters' traits from actions and dialogues and support their answers with concrete details from the text." The actual task required students only to list the traits of the characters (e.g., cross and greedy), however, and provide extremely limited evidence from the text to support their responses (isolated quotes from the story). For this reason, these learning goals were considered to be only somewhat aligned with the assignment. If, for example, students had written an essay describing the character with supporting evidence from the text for each trait, then this assignment would have received a higher score for this dimension. The excerpt of student work that follows was considered by the teacher to be of medium quality for the class.

> *Scrooge at the Beginning of the Story*: Cross, Greedy, Doesn't like Christmas, Unhappy, "There's a penny saved. Lantern's gone out. No matter. A candle saved." "If they would rather die, they had better do it and decrease the surplus population. That is not my affair. My business is."
>
> *Scrooge at the End of the Story*: Generous, Kind, Merry, Loving and affectionate, "I'll give you half a crown." "God bless everyone!" "Oh, tell me I am not too late." "I will not shut out the lesson that they teach."

Tenth Grade

For this assignment students read a series of journal entries written by a soldier during World War I. The teacher's goals for this assignment were that students "become familiar with, summarize, and learn to analyze primary source historical material." Because students read excerpts from the soldier's journal, the task was aligned with the teacher's first goal that students become familiar with primary source historical material.

The actual assignment, however, only required students to summarize the journal entries and answer a series of factual, low-inference questions. Students did not engage in any analysis of the entries. For this reason, the learning goals were considered to be only partially aligned with the assignment. The following is an excerpt of student work:

1. *In your own words, write about what happened each day as described by the American solider in his journal entries.*

   September 11—They are ready for the battle and feel prepared for anything.

   September 12—The battle started. The enemy surrendered and left behind a great deal of equipment.

   September 13—They progressed toward their destination No rest from last night.

2. *Why do you think the soldiers did not move for more than five miles?* The allies lost 620,000 French and British troops in just five miles.

3. *Why do we celebrate Veteran's Day on November 11?* To honor the soldiers who fought for our country. This was the day the fighting officially ended.

LEVEL 3: GOALS FOR STUDENT LEARNING ARE FULLY ALIGNED WITH THE ASSIGNMENT TASK

At the highest level of quality the teacher's goals for student learning are completely realized in the assignment task. The goals are clear and specific and fully reflected in what students are asked to do (see Table 8.1).

Third Grade

The highest score for this dimension is illustrated in the following assignment based on the book *By the Great Horn Spoon* by Sid Fleischman. This book is about a young boy, Jack, and his butler friend, Praiseworthy, who seek their fortunes in California during the Gold Rush period. The teacher's learning goals for this assignment were that students "learn to use a Venn diagram to help them compare and contrast two characters

(Jack and Praiseworthy) from the story. I wanted them to focus on salient differences and similarities between the two characters—not just that they were friends."

To prepare for the assignment, students worked in small groups to complete Venn diagrams that mapped out the qualities of each character, as well as overlapping similarities. Students then wrote three paragraphs, the first describing Praiseworthy, the second describing Jack, and the last paragraph comparing the two characters. The following is an excerpt from a student's essay:

By the Great Horn Spoon

Jack and Praiseworthy are similar in that they both want to help Aunt Arabella because she is going to lose her house. They both want to find gold and they both work hard. They are both decent and nice people. They are different because Praiseworthy is an adult and Jack is a child. Praiseworthy is more educated than Jack. He always figures out how to solve their problems. Praiseworthy would rather stay at home, and Jack likes to see different places.

This assignment was given the highest score for this dimension, since the teacher's goals for the task were completely reflected in the assignment task. Students created and used Venn diagrams to map out the qualities of the two main characters, and they described the characters in three-paragraph responses. The differences and similarities between the characters also focused on some salient similarities and differences between the main characters (e.g., that they were different ages, that Praiseworthy was more educated, and that they were similar in their desire to help Aunt Arabella). For these reasons, the assignment received a 3 for the alignment of the teacher's learning goals and assignment task.

Seventh Grade

A seventh-grade assignment that received the highest score for this dimension was one in which students analyzed an article from an environmental magazine. The teacher's learning goals for this assignment were that students "analyze an environmental problem, identify the cause of the problem, citing facts and details, and present possible workable solutions to the problem." Analyzing a problem and posing possible workable solutions are high-level goals. To achieve these goals, the teacher had the students write a persuasive letter to an environmental agency describing the specifics of the problem and outlining possible solutions. To support the realization of these goals in the students' work, the teacher had students review each other's letters and provided them with a rubric that guided them to consider whether or not the author had expressed concern about the problem, adequately described the causes of the problem (including who, what, where, when, and why) and posed reasonable solutions. The following is an excerpt from a student's letter for this assignment:

> To Whom it May Concern,
>
>   I am writing to express concern about the thousands of sea turtles killed annually in shrimp nets. . . .
>
>   . . . One solution to this problem is a Turtle Excluder Device which is a trap door which allows air-breathing turtles to swim through the nets free of harm. Using a Turtle Excluder Device reduces the number of turtles who die in shrimp nets by 97 percent. Another solution would be to not let fishermen cast their nets where sea turtles live.

Tenth Grade

A tenth-grade assignment that illustrates the highest score for this dimension, is one in which students wrote an essay based on the poem "A Black Man Talks of Reaping" by Arna Bontemps. The teacher's learning goals for this assignment were that students "be able to recognize literary techniques used in poetry. They would then be able to analyze the poem and in a formal essay explain how the techniques used in the poem (tone, hyperbole, and symbolism) enhanced and supported the theme of the poem. Supporting quotes from the poem were required."

Students read and discussed several poems in class and each day responded to a journal question based on the theme of the poem they had read. Students then were given the following prompt to write their essays:

> Read the poem "A Black Man Talks of Reaping" and determine the main idea (theme) of the poem. Then, in a well-developed essay (introduction and thesis statement, body, and conclusion), discuss how the language techniques used in the poem (tone, hyperbole, and symbolism) enhanced the poem's theme. Make sure to use examples from the poem to illustrate each of these techniques.

As with the previous assignment, this assignment received a high score for this dimension because the teacher's goals for student learning overlapped completely with what students were asked to do in their essays. In other words, the writing prompt furthered the teacher's learning goals with regard to analyzing the poem by showing how the author's use of very specific literary techniques furthered the theme, and students were also reminded to use quotes from the poem to support their answers. The following is an excerpt from a student's essay that the teacher considered to be of medium quality for the assignment for the class:

"A Black Man Talks of Reaping"
The tone of the poem shows that this man is afraid because people are prejudiced against him. "Within my heart the fear that wind of fowl would take the grain away." You get the feeling that he is worried that the wind could easily take away all he's worked for. In reality for all his hard work, all he will get in return is "only what the hand can hold" or just enough to get by. Due to this man's color he is not given what he really deserves.

SUMMARY

One of the challenges of creating high-quality assignment tasks is making sure that they fully reflect the goals for student learning. In other words, it is important to make sure that students have the opportunity to learn the specific skills intended by the teacher. For example, if a teacher's goals are that students learn to analyze and interpret text, then it is important that the assignment task facilitate the learning of these skills as opposed to other skills (e.g., summarizing). Aligning assignment tasks with higher-level goals is more challenging than it might seem, especially since there appears to be some room for interpretation regarding the implementation of critical thinking skills. Additionally, in order to have a high degree of alignment between the learning goals and the task it is important that the learning goals be clear and specific. Just about any type of assignment task could be aligned with a broad goal (e.g., that students learn "comprehension skills") and would not necessarily further students' learning. Furthermore, this could hinder student learning by limiting the amount of information they receive with regard to their progress toward specific learning goals. This idea will be discussed further in Chapter 9.

QUESTIONS TO GUIDE REFLECTION AND ANALYSIS OF THE ALIGNMENT OF THE LEARNING GOALS AND THE ASSIGNMENT TASK

1. Were the goals for student learning furthered in the assignment task? For example, if the goal was for students to develop their analytical-thinking skills, were students required to apply analytical skills to complete the assignment?
2. How specific was the alignment between the goals for student learning and the assignment task?

9

DID STUDENTS RECEIVE FEEDBACK ON WHAT THEY WERE SUPPOSED TO LEARN? ALIGNING THE LEARNING GOALS WITH THE GRADING CRITERIA

The final step in developing an assignment is to make sure that students are provided with information about their progress toward the learning goals. The grading criteria for an assignment and the comments teachers make on students' papers, therefore, should reflect—or be aligned with—the goals for student learning. For example, if a teacher's goals are that students learn to "support their statements with evidence from the text," the assessment criteria for grading students' work ideally would include clear and specific information about how much and what types of evidence the teacher is looking for in students' writing. Or if a teacher's learning goal is that students "evaluate a text" the assessment criteria for that assignment would ideally specify features of a high-quality evaluation.

While this may appear to be self-evident, as, perhaps, the alignment of learning goals and assignment tasks may be, my research in classrooms indicates that teachers' learning goals often are not reflected in their criteria for assessing students' work (see, for example, Clare & Aschbacher, 2001). Providing students with feedback about their comprehension of a text is a difficult task, and it is made harder by the fact that few rubrics exist for assessing students' responses to literature. Many more rubrics seem to exist that focus on the quality of students' general writing skills. Hopefully, in time, more rubrics for assessing responses to literature assignments in classrooms will be created, and this may assist teachers in aligning their learning goals with their assessment criteria in this area.

Analagously to Chapter 8, which focused on the alignment of the assignment activity and learning goals, this chapter provides support for aligning the goals for student learning with an assignment's grading criteria. The clearer, more specific, and detailed a teacher's learning goals and assessment criteria are for an assignment, the more precisely they potentially could overlap with each other. To receive the highest score on this dimension, therefore, the learning goals and assessment criteria would be clear, specific, and detailed and the learning goals would be completely reflected in the assessment criteria.

LEVEL 1: THE GRADING CRITERIA ARE NOT ALIGNED WITH THE LEARNING GOALS

At the lowest level of quality a teacher's learning goals and the criteria for assessing students' work are not aligned (see Table 9.1). In other words, there is no evidence that the teacher's goals for what students are to learn as a result of completing the assignment task are reflected in the grading criteria.

Third Grade

The lowest score for this dimension is illustrated in the following third-grade assignment. For this assignment students read *The True Story of the Three Little Pigs* by Jon Scieszka and wrote a letter arguing that the wolf was either guilty or innocent of eating two of the pigs and destroying their houses. The teacher's goals for the assignment were that

Table 9.1   Aligning the Grading Criteria With the Goals for Student Learning

Level 1	Level 2	Level 3
The grading criteria and the learning goals are not aligned.	The grading criteria and the learning goals are partially aligned or are aligned at a very general level.	The grading criteria and the learning goals are detailed and fully aligned.

students "learn to compare and contrast point of view, make predictions, and justify their opinions."

A rubric that focused on the quality of the students' writing was used to assess students' work. The criteria for assessing students' work were

A = Excellent. The writing is fluent and articulate. None, or very few spelling errors.
B = Good. Good fluency and articulation. Few spelling errors.
C = Satisfactory. Work completed. Some articulation and fluency.
D = Not Satisfactory. Work incomplete, difficult to understand.

This assignment was given the lowest score for this dimension because none of the teacher's goals for student learning were reflected in these criteria. The teacher's goals focused on important skills—comparing and contrasting, predicting, and justifying opinions—that have the potential to deepen students' knowledge of the text and develop their thinking skills. The grading criteria, in contrast, only focused on the general quality of students' writing, not the development of these higher-level skills. This assignment would have received a higher score for this dimension if students had been provided with grading criteria that included information about how to measure their progress toward the attainment of these skills.

Seventh Grade

For this assignment students wrote a summary of a short story they had read in class. The teacher's goals for this assignment were that students "comprehend the elements of the story and learn how to write a detailed summary." The teacher assessed the quality of students' work, however, solely on the basis of students' grammar skills. Specifically, in the teacher's words, "middle level students had severe errors in English grammar while high students had less errors and wrote more." Because the quality of students' summaries, specifically the amount of and type of detail they included in their writing was not addressed, this assignment also was considered to illustrate the lowest score for this dimension.

Tenth Grade

A tenth-grade assignment that also received a 1 for the alignment of the learning goals and the assessment criteria was one in which students wrote an evaluation of a book of their choice. The teacher's learning goals were that students "learn to think critically and develop their evaluative and persuasive writing skills." The criteria used to assess the quality of students' work, however, focused on the general quality of students' writing. Specifically, the teacher used the following rubric to grade students' writing:

A = Writing is clear, clear and compelling thesis statement, five paragraphs with topic sentences, all paragraphs indented, few grammar and spelling errors.

B = Clear thesis statement, five paragraphs with topic sentences, all paragraphs indented, some grammar and spelling errors.

C = Thesis statement may be missing, five paragraphs, many grammar and spelling errors.

D = Writing is difficult to understand or essay is incomplete.

F = Assignment is missing.

Because these criteria focused almost exclusively on the general features of a five-paragraph essay and did not overlap with the teacher's goal that the students develop their evaluative and persuasive writing skills and learn to think critically about what they were reading, this assignment received the lowest score for this dimension.

LEVEL 2: THE GRADING CRITERIA ARE PARTIALLY ALIGNED WITH THE LEARNING GOALS

At the next level of quality the grading criteria for the assignment and the teacher's learning goals are partially aligned (see Table 9.1). This means that some, but not all, of the learning goals are reflected in the grading criteria for the assignment. Alternatively, assignments that receive a 2 for this dimension could be aligned at a very general level only. As described in the previous chapters, the learning goals and assignment grading criteria developed by many teachers lack detail and specificity. It is possible for learning goals and grading criteria that are stated in very broad terms to be aligned, but this alignment would not be very specific. Examples of assignments that scored a 2 for these different reasons are presented here.

Third Grade

For this assignment students wrote an evaluation of a short story from their basal readers. The teacher's learning goals for this assignment were that students "learn to write persuasively and clearly and include concrete examples from the story." The following rubric was used to assess students' work:

4 = Writing is fluent and clear, proper paragraph format is followed, and ideas are supported by at least three details from the story.

3 = Proper paragraph format is followed, and ideas are supported by at least three details from the story.

2 = Proper paragraph format is mostly followed, and ideas are supported by at least two details from the story.

1 = Proper paragraph format is not followed, and ideas are not supported by details from the story.

This assignment received a 2 for this dimension since most, but not all, of the learning goals were reflected in the grading criteria. Specifically, the grading rubric includes information about the number of details students are to include in their writing, and it focuses somewhat on clarity (to receive the highest score) but does not include information about students' skill at writing persuasively. If the grading criteria had specified different degrees of quality with regard to students' persuasive writing skills (e.g., clear statement of opinion and facts from story to support specific points) then this assignment likely would have received a higher score for this dimension.

Seventh Grade

For this assignment students read *Freaky Friday* by Mary Rodgers and compared the book with its movie adaptation. The learning goals for this assignment were that students "make comparisons between the book and the movie." The assessment criteria for the assignment also were fairly general. Specifically, according to the teacher, student work that received high scores had "many similarities and differences recorded between the book and the movie." Student work that received medium scores had only "some comparisons between the book and the movie." Because these goals and grading criteria were aligned but were not especially elaborated or detailed, this assignment also was considered to illustrate a 2 for this dimension.

Tenth Grade

For this tenth-grade assignment, students read *Fahrenheit 451* by Ray Bradbury and wrote an essay comparing the society portrayed in the book with society today. The teacher's goals for this assignment were that students "learn to write a compare and contrast essay and look critically at our current society and make judgments about the state of it. I want them to be able to express their ideas clearly in a five-paragraph essay format and support their answers with concrete details from the text." To assess students' work, the teacher used a five-point rubric. The criteria for obtaining an A on this assignment for both content and organization is shown in Table 9.2.

Table 9.2   Fahrenheit 451 Assignment Grading Criteria Example

Grade	Content	Organization
A	Clearly expresses ideas to an intended audience and conveys a distinct point of view. Ideas are fully developed and integrated and are supported with concrete details from the text.	Topic is adhered to and writing is logically organized. The writing has a clear introduction, thesis statement, body, and conclusion. Proper paragraph structure is followed, with a topic sentence, at least two commentaries for every concrete detail, and a concluding sentence.
B	Clearly expresses ideas to an intended audience and conveys a distinct point of view. Ideas are appropriate and are supported with concrete details from the text.	Topic is adhered to and writing is logically organized. The writing has a clear thesis statement, body, and conclusion. Proper paragraph structure is followed, with a topic sentence, at least two commentaries for every concrete detail, and a concluding sentence.
C	Ideas are appropriate and supported with some concrete details. May contain a minor factual error.	Topic is adhered to and writing is organized into paragraphs. Writing has a sense of an introduction, thesis, body, and conclusion. Commentary is not supported by concrete details.
D	Limited development of ideas and use of concrete details. May contain obvious factual errors and omissions.	Topic is not adhered to; writing is unclear and disorganized. No clear sense of an introduction, body, or conclusion. Lack of commentary and concrete details.

This assignment received a 2 for this dimension because only some of the teacher's goals (i.e., that students write a well-organized five-paragraph essay and include concrete details from the text) were reflected in the grading criteria. Other aspects of the teacher's goals, pertaining specifically to the content of the text (i.e., that students compare and contrast and make judgments about the society in which we live) were not included in the grading criteria. This assignment would have received a higher score for this dimension if the teacher had specified levels of quality with regard to students' comparisons and judgments of the novel.

LEVEL 3: THE GRADING CRITERIA ARE FULLY ALIGNED WITH THE LEARNING GOALS

At the highest level of quality the learning goals for the assignment are fully reflected in the grading criteria used to assess students' work (see Table 9.1). Additionally, the learning goals and assessment criteria are sufficiently detailed that the alignment between them can occur at a fairly specific level.

Third Grade

For this third-grade assignment students wrote a retelling of *My Life with the Wave* by Catherine Cowan. The teacher's goals for this assignment were that students, "learn to write a detailed and accurate retelling of a story (beginning, middle, and end) and include all the story elements (characters, setting, plot, conflict, and resolution). I also wanted them to discuss the 'moral' of the story."

These are the criteria to obtain the highest score on the five-point rubric that the teacher used to assess students' work:

5 = Retells the beginning, middle and end of the story accurately in own words and includes essential details, includes all story elements, synthesizes text into key theme, moral or deeper meaning.

This assignment received the highest score for this dimension because the teacher's learning goals (that students include all story elements and essential details and describe the moral of the story in their retellings) were all included in the rubric used to grade students' work. Additionally, the goals and the assessment criteria were sufficiently detailed so these two elements could be aligned fairly specifically.

Seventh Grade

For this seventh-grade assignment students wrote an evaluation of a book of their choice. The teacher's learning goals for the assignment were that students "write a five-paragraph essay evaluating a book of their choice. I wanted them to describe the criteria they used to judge their book and support their answers with pertinent details and examples." To assess students' work the teacher used a four-point rubric, with the following being the criteria for the highest score:

- Overall evaluation of subject is stated with reasons
- Examples from text used to convincingly support judgment
- Strong conclusion reinforces argument
- Correct five-paragraph essay format followed with smooth transitions
- Minimal errors in grammar, punctuation, language use, or spelling

This assignment received the highest score for this dimension because the learning goals were fully aligned with the assessment criteria. Specifically, the teacher's learning goals that students write a five-paragraph essay, state their evaluation criteria, and support their answers with examples from the book they chose were all included in the rubric the teacher used to assess students' work.

Tenth Grade

For this tenth-grade assignment, students analyzed a speech from Shakespeare's *The Tragedy of Julius Caesar*. The teacher's learning goals for this assignment were that students "learn to do a close reading of a text and analyze the persuasive content of a speech by identifying specific rhetorical devices with examples. I also wanted them to display mastery of the eight-sentence paragraph and five-paragraph essay format."

The rubric shown in Table 9.3 was used to grade students' essays (students received a separate grade for each dimension).

Table 9.3   The Tragedy of Julius Caesar Assignment Grading Criteria Example

Grade	A	B	C	D
Content	The essay accurately identifies rhetorical devices, and includes insightful commentary, as well as excellent use of supporting details.	The essay accurately identifies rhetorical devices and includes sufficient use of supporting details.	The essay identifies some rhetorical devices but lacks supporting details and perhaps contains some factual inaccuracies.	The essay does not fulfill the purposes of the assignment, and the writing may be off topic.
Organization	The essay indicates a student's mastery of the eight-paragraph and five-paragraph essay format (including thesis, supporting paragraphs, and conclusion) and shows a skillful use of transitions.	The essay indicates a student's mastery of the eight-paragraph and five-paragraph essay format but has limited use of transitions.	Application of eight-paragraph or five-paragraph essay format is problematic.	Application of eight-paragraph or five-paragraph essay format is problematic.
Language Use	The essay includes strong word choices, concise sentences, excellent variety of sentence structure, and few if any mechanical errors.	The essay includes strong word choices, a good variety of sentence structure, and only mechanical errors that do not detract from meaning.	The essay exhibits adequate word choices, limited sentence-structure variety, and several mechanical errors.	Word choices are poor, and the writing is difficult to understand.

Each of the teacher's learning goals was reflected in the assessment criteria, and these goals and criteria were sufficiently detailed to allow for alignment at a more specific level. For these reasons, this assignment, too, received a 3 for the alignment of the goals for student learning and the assessment criteria.

SUMMARY

The final step in creating an assignment is to make sure that the learning goals for the assignment are fully reflected in the grading criteria. Additionally, the learning goals and the criteria for assessing students' work should be clear and detailed so that the alignment between these two elements can occur at a specific level, which is important for allowing students to measure their progress toward a teacher's goals. If the learning goals, for example, are broadly stated (e.g., if the teacher's goals are that students learn "reading comprehension skills") or if the grading criteria are vague and general, then the alignment between these elements likely would be less meaningful in terms of supporting student learning, because the information they received from the assessment process would be less focused and precise.

QUESTIONS TO GUIDE REFLECTION AND ANALYSIS OF THE ALIGNMENT OF THE GRADING CRITERIA AND THE LEARNING GOALS

1. Were the goals for student learning reflected in the grading criteria? For example, if the goal was for students to develop their analytical thinking skills, were students assessed on the quality of their analyses?
2. How specific was the alignment between the goals for student learning and the grading criteria?

10

PUTTING IT ALL TOGETHER: ASSIGNMENT QUALITY ANALYSIS IN ACTION

In this chapter, the process of analyzing assignment quality is illustrated using the nine dimensions presented in the previous chapters. As described in the introduction, the vast majority of assignments are neither all good nor all bad; instead, most assignments have elements that are strong and elements that could be improved. For example, a teacher could assign students a great book to read but might not develop a writing activity that supports students in writing about the rich content of the book. Another teacher might assign students a challenging, exciting task but not provide students with high-quality feedback on their efforts. In both cases the potential for student learning is limited, though the prescription for "improving" these assignments would be very different.

In the following sections the process teachers might engage in, alone or with colleagues, to analyze the unique strengths and weaknesses of their assignments is modeled with six assignments from the third, seventh, and tenth grades. A story retelling and an assignment requiring students to make a personal connection with a text, done in a third-grade classroom, are analyzed. Also evaluated are a book evaluation and a descriptive-essay task from seventh grade, and tenth-grade assignments requiring students to answer a series of comprehension questions and write an analytic essay.

STORY RETELLING: THIRD GRADE

For this assignment students wrote a retelling of the book *The Hundred Dresses* by Eleanor Estes. The teacher's learning goals for this assignment were that students "be able to retell the events in the story and grasp the essential conflict, that is, to understand why Maddie did not defend Wanda and make a judgment about that. I also wanted them to support their answers with many details from the story." The following is an excerpt of student work for this assignment considered by the teacher to be of high quality for the class:

The Hundred Dresses

This story is about a girl named Maddie. She and her friend tease a girl named Wanda. They tease her because she says she has 100 dresses but she only wears one dress. They tease her so much she leaves the school. Then Wanda won a prize because she drew 100 dresses. Maddie and her friend Peggy wrote her a letter and Wanda gave them a picture of a dress.

Maddie feels bad in the story because she did not stick up for Wanda. She didn't say anything when the girls were picking on her. Maddie was afraid that they would start on her because she was poor. She didn't want the girls to know that she wore Peggy's old clothes.

I think that Maddie should have helped Wanda. I think that she should have apologized to Wanda so she would have felt better.

To assess the quality of students' work, the teacher used a four-point rubric. The criteria for the highest score are shown below:

- Beginning, middle, and end accurately described
- Student accurately describes Maddie's conflict in the story
- At least three paragraphs
- Answers supported with many story details
- No (or very minor) spelling and punctuation errors

According to the teacher, she discussed these criteria with students in class in advance of their completing the assignment.

The specific assignment directions given to students were as follows:

The Hundred Dresses

You will be writing a retelling of the story, *The Hundred Dresses*. Your essay should be at least three paragraphs long and should follow proper paragraph form. You also should use proper punctuation and spelling.

In the first paragraph tell the reader what the story is about. Make sure that you describe the beginning, middle, and end of the story.

In the second paragraph, write about why Maddie did not defend Wanda and how this made her feel. Remember to include details from the story.

In the final paragraph state your opinion about what Maddie did. Was she wrong to not defend Wanda? Was sending the letter to Wanda a good enough apology?

Students wrote a first draft, received feedback from their teacher and a peer, and then revised their work based on these comments. The following is a discussion of this assignment following the dimensions outlined in the previous chapters.

Engaging With Substantive Academic Content

For this assignment students read *The Hundred Dresses* by Eleanor Estes. As described earlier, this book is about a girl, Maddie, whose very popular and wealthy best friend leads the other students in teasing a poorer girl, Wanda, in the class. This teasing eventually causes Wanda to leave the school. The story centers on Maddie's compliance in the teasing, born from her own fears of being teased, and her guilt over not speaking out on Wanda's behalf. This book contains a wealth of complex ideas and themes that could support substantive discussions and writing assignments. For example, the main character, Maddie, is sympathetic but by no means perfect. She suffers genuine remorse over her actions, but she neither defends Wanda nor apologizes to her. Students could write about why certain students—in this case, Wanda—are chosen to be the target of bullying. Or, as with the assignment the teacher gave to the third-grade class, students could write about why Maddie did not defend Wanda. Because the story contains both complex characters and ideas that could support meaningful discussion and writing, this assignment received the highest score, a 3, for the quality of the text.

Setting Clear and Rigorous Goals for Student Learning

The teacher's goals for this assignment were fairly detailed and included a strong focus on the content she wanted students to comprehend from the story. For this reason these goals received the highest score, a 4, for this dimension.

Applying Complex Thinking Skills: Analyzing and Interpreting a Text

In addition to reading a high-quality text, the assignment task (i.e., what students were actually asked to write about) guided students to engage with the rich content of the story. In addition to summarizing the events in the story, students were guided to write about the dilemma faced by the main character and why she allowed herself to be complicit in the teasing. They also were asked to evaluate the character's behavior and support their answers with evidence from the text. While students could perhaps have provided more evidence from the text to support their answers (as evidenced in the essay excerpt provided) and perhaps received more guidance for how best to do this, it is clear that the assignment task provided them with an opportunity to think deeply about what they read. For this reason, this assignment received the highest score, a 4, for this dimension.

Developing Clear and Rigorous Criteria to Assess Students' Work

This assignment received a high score, a 4, for the clarity and content of the grading criteria. As already shown, the different dimensions of quality are defined for each level of success, and they focus on students' engagement with the primary moral dilemma and overall meaning of the text. How the teacher defined work of high, medium, and low quality is clear, and these criteria, although not written in language that would be accessible to young students, still contain information that could potentially help students improve the quality of their work, provided these ideas were communicated to students in a way that was understandable to them.

Communicating the Criteria for High-Quality Work to Students

The teacher reported that she discussed her grading criteria with students in class in advance of their completing the assignment. For this reason, this assignment received a 2 for this dimension. To receive a higher score, the teacher would have supported this discussion with a written version of the criteria (e.g., a posted criteria chart students could refer to, or models of high-quality work), and would have guided students to use these criteria to produce or revise their work.

Providing Clear and Rigorous Written Assignment Directions

The assignment directions provided students with information about what they were to do and include in their essays to receive a high score for this assignment. For this reason, this assignment received the highest score, a 3, for this dimension.

Providing Content-Specific Feedback on Drafts of Students' Work

Students produced two drafts for this assignment, one that was edited by the teacher and a peer, and then a final draft. The feedback students received on their first draft focused primarily on correcting their grammar, punctuation, and spelling. Students also received a few comments, however, that focused on improving the content of their essays. For example, after a student wrote, "She didn't say anything when the girls were picking on her," on her first draft the teacher wrote, "Why didn't she say anything?" On the second draft the student then added the following sentence, "Maddie was afraid that they would start on her because she was poor and wore Peggy's old clothes." Because students received at least some degree of feedback that focused on the content of their writing, this assignment received a 3 for this dimension.

Aligning the Goals for Student Learning With the Assignment Task

The teacher's goals for this assignment were reflected in the assignment task. Students were guided to describe the essential conflict in the story and support their responses with examples from the text. For this reason, this assignment therefore illustrates the highest score, a 3, for this dimension.

Aligning the Grading Criteria With the Goals for Student Learning

As described above, the rubric the teacher used to assess students' work included a focus on getting students to understand the main conflict in the story and support their responses with examples from the story. These criteria were reflected in the actual assignment task and directions to students. This assignment, therefore, received the highest score, a 3, for this dimension.

Summary of the Strengths and Weaknesses of the Story Retelling Assignment

Overall, this was a very strong assignment. Students read an excellent text and were guided to engage with the rich thematic content of the story in their writing. The teacher's learning goals focused on students grasping the deeper meaning of the story, and this was reflected in the design of the assignment task and in the criteria for assessing students' work. The teacher also made her performance expectations clear to students in the form of fairly detailed assignment directions and grading criteria.

While strong overall, this assignment could have been even better if the teacher had focused more on students' use of more evidence from the text to support their writing. Additionally, while the teacher provided some content-level feedback on their first drafts, an additional draft, with more attention to students' use of story details to support their responses, likely would have improved the quality of students' writing. Being provided with models of high-quality work in advance of completing their essays—in addition to discussing the criteria in class—also might have supported students in producing stronger essays.

PERSONAL CONNECTION: THIRD GRADE

For this assignment students read *The Watsons Go to Birmingham—1963* by Christopher Paul Curtis and wrote a single draft of a one-paragraph narrative connecting an event in the story to their personal experience. The teacher's goal for this assignment was for students to "learn to connect personally to what they read." The following is an example of student work for this assignment considered by the teacher to be of high quality for the class:

The Watsons Go to Birmingham: 1963
In the book it says that Rufus is still mad at Kenny for laughing at him. Kenny feels bad and tries to make it up to Rufus by playing with him. But Rufus was still mad at Kenny and Kenny started to feel bad about what he did. This made me think about how Anthony might feel if I laughed at him.

The teacher did not use a formal rubric to assess students' work for this assignment. Instead she described her criteria for differentiating between low, medium, and high student performance on the students' compositions:

Low performance = a student wasn't able to make a thoughtful connection or elaborate on their thinking.
Medium performance = a student wasn't clear and specific in their examples, did not elaborate on their thinking.
High performance = a student gave thoughtful responses, many examples from text.

The teacher did not give students a written copy of the assignment directions. She also did not provide students with a copy of her grading criteria or models of high-quality work in advance of their completing the assignment.

Engaging With Substantive Academic Content

The text for this assignment, *The Watsons Go to Birmingham— 1963*, is an excellent choice. This story is about a ten-year-old boy, Kenny, and his family. This book contains fully rounded characters and complex themes regarding the vagaries of friendship and sibling relationships. Additionally, this book addresses racism and contains excellent historical information about the civil rights movement. Because this book includes so much that can be written about and discussed this assignment received the highest score, a 3, for this dimension.

Setting Clear and Rigorous Goals for Student Learning

The teacher's learning goal for this assignment, that students "learn to connect personally to what they read," is quite vague and nonspecific with regard to content. For this reason, this assignment was considered to illustrate the lowest score, a 1, for the clarity and content of the learning goals. If the teacher had been more specific about what she intended students to learn through completing the task—for example, the specific messages and themes in the text that she wanted students to engage with—then this assignment would have received a higher score for this dimension.

Applying Complex Thinking Skills: Analyzing and Interpreting a Text

While the text for this assignment was excellent, the actual task students completed fell short in terms of supporting students to apply complex thinking skills. Students chose a specific part of the text from the chapter they had read in class and answered the prompt, "This reminds me of. . . ." Looking at the range of samples of student work for this assignment, it is clear that the connections students made were not very developed. In the chapter students had read in class, the main character, Kenny, who is often picked on and teased by his classmates, makes friends with another boy, Rufus, and Rufus's brother, who are new to the school. Rufus and his younger brother are poorer than many of the other children and are teased because they share the few clothes that they own. Out of a sense of relief that he is not the one being singled out for teasing for a change, Kenny laughs along with the other children and does not defend his new friends. As a result, Rufus and his brother refuse to play with Kenny until Kenny, with the help of his mother, eventually apologizes.

Similar to the theme in *The Hundred Dresses* by Eleanor Estes, the chapter students read addresses the problem of being teased, as well as the consequences of not standing up for others who are targeted for abuse. The assignment, however, did not guide students to focus on these essential issues. Instead, as evidenced in the directions to students and the following examples of student work, students chose fairly random selections from the reading with which to make a personal connection. For example, one student, whose work was considered to be of medium quality for the class, chose to write about the section where Kenny's mother makes lunch for the boys. This is a fairly trivial event in the story. Another student whose work was considered to be of high quality for the class (see the excerpt of the student essay) wrote about the fight between Kenny and Rufus, but without much depth or detail. Additionally, his personal connection ("This made me think about how Anthony might feel") is not elaborated. It is therefore not clear from the student's writing whether or not he truly understood the deeper-level content of the story. For this reason, because students made tangential connections and did not connect with the deeper ideas in the chapter, this assignment received a 2 for the application of complex thinking skills.

This assignment would have received a higher score for this dimension if students had been guided to write personal connections that gave them access to the meaningful content of the story. For example, students could have been asked to describe the crisis in Kenny and Rufus's friendship—why Kenny did not stand up for Rufus, and why Rufus was hurt by Kenny's behavior. The students then could have written about a time that they were teased (like Rufus) or had a friend who was teased (like Kenny) and what they did about it. This assignment also would have been stronger if students had been guided to include more details from the text in their writing and had written more than single-paragraph responses.

Developing Clear and Rigorous Criteria to Assess Students' Work

These criteria received a 2 for their clarity and specificity because they were fairly general and would not provide a great deal of information to students about what they would need to do, or include in their writing, to receive a high score on the task. For example, it is not clear what the teacher was looking for in terms of "thoughtful" student responses, or what she meant by students elaborating on their thinking. These criteria would have received a higher score for this dimension if the teacher had been more specific and detailed in terms of her expectations for high-quality work, and, as described earlier, if the criteria had focused on students' discussion of the salient themes and ideas in the text and on them supporting their responses with details from the story.

Communicating the Criteria for High-Quality Work to Students

The teacher reported that she discussed the criteria for high-quality work with students in advance of their completing the assignment, but she did not provide them with access to a written version of the criteria students could refer to when completing their work. For this reason, this assignment was considered to illustrate a score of 2 for this dimension. It is possible that the quality of student work might have improved if the teacher also had provided students with models of high-quality work, and a much more specific version of the grading criteria and assignment directions she had created.

Providing Clear and Rigorous Written Assignment Directions

The teacher did not provide students with written directions for this assignment so it was not possible to assess this dimension.

Providing Content-Specific Feedback on Drafts of Students' Work

Students wrote only one draft of their compositions so it was not possible to assess the quality of the feedback the teacher provided to students on drafts of their compositions.

Aligning the Goals for Student Learning With the Assignment Task

As described earlier, the teacher's goal for this assignment—that students learn to connect personally with what they read—was not very specific and elaborated. Many different kinds of personal-connection assignments could have fulfilled these goals. For this reason, the teacher's learning goal was considered to be aligned with the assignment task at a very general level and therefore received a 2 for this dimension.

Aligning the Grading Criteria With the Goals for Student Learning

The grading criteria for this assignment, that students write "thoughtful" responses and provide examples from the text, were aligned only at a very general level with the teacher's learning goals that students connect personally to what they read. For this reason, this assignment illustrates a score of 2 for this dimension.

Summary of the Strengths and Weaknesses of the Personal Connection Assignment

As with *The Hundred Dresses* assignment, the great strength of this assignment was in the teacher's choice of text for students to read. Connecting personally to what you read can be a very powerful way to help students engage with the content of a story. For example, students could have been asked to write about which character they identified with most and why, using examples from the story and from their personal life to understand the dynamics of bullying. The structure of this assignment, however, did not support students' efforts make a personal connection with the text that provided them with access to the meaningful content of the chapter. The connections made by students were mostly tangential and lacked examples and detail from the stories. The lack of clarity and specificity with regard to student learning was reflected in the broad and general learning goals and assessment criteria. Developing a more explicit idea of what ideas or themes from the chapter she wanted students to engage with, and sharing these expectations with students in the form of clearer and more detailed assignment directions and assessment criteria, likely would have improved the quality of the students' work. Providing students with feedback on early drafts of their work and giving them the opportunity to incorporate this feedback into their final drafts also likely would have improved the quality of students' essays.

BOOK EVALUATION: SEVENTH GRADE

For this assignment students wrote an evaluation of a book of their choice. One student, whose work is described below, evaluated *Pokemon the First Movie: Mewtwo Strikes Back* by Tracey West, which is a book from a series on the Pokemon characters. The teacher's learning goals for this assignment were as follows:

> I wanted students to write a five-paragraph essay evaluating a book of their choice. Specifically, I wanted them to develop their skills at writing persuasively. I wanted them to learn to write clear theses statements and [support] their arguments with examples from the text.

The following is an excerpt of student work for this assignment that the teacher considered to be of medium quality for the class:

Mewto Strickes [sic] Back
The book I read was [*Pokemon the First Movie*] *Mewtwo Strikes Back*. I like this book a lot. I think that a seventh-grader would like this book because it is very cool and exciting. This book was cool because Mewtwo cloned the real pokemon and had to fight against the cloned pokemon who was stronger. In the beginning of the story Mewtwo had on armor on full of wires to make him stronger. Mewtwo thought that he was an experiment.

Then Mewtwo said "You created me to run tests on me?" Mewtwo was really angry and destroyed the lab. Another reason I thought it was cool was because Mewtwo used his powerful psychic ability to destroy the lab.

The teacher used a rubric to grade students' work. It was necessary to meet these criteria to earn the highest score:

- Criteria upon which text is evaluated is stated in introduction
- Overall evaluation of subject is stated with reasons
- Examples from text used to convincingly support judgment
- Strong conclusion reinforces argument
- Correct five-paragraph essay format followed with smooth transitions
- Minimal errors in grammar, punctuation, language use, or spelling

The teacher reported that she discussed her criteria for grading their work with students in advance of their completing their evaluations but that she did not provide students with a copy of the rubric or written assignment directions. Students wrote two drafts of their essays and received edits to the first draft that focused solely on improving their grammar, punctuation, and spelling.

Engaging With Substantive Academic Content

In contrast to the previously discussed assignments in this chapter, the text for this assignment did not contain much academic content, or characters and themes that were complex enough to support meaningful discussions and writing. *Mewtwo Strikes Back* by Tracey West is one in a series chronicling the adventures of the Pokemon characters. While this is a chapter book with some plot complexity, the story does not contain rich characters, complex themes, or expose students to meaningful learning in other content areas. For these reasons, this assignment received a basic score, a 2, for this dimension.

Setting Clear and Rigorous Goals for Student Learning

The teacher's goals were clear in terms of what she wanted students to learn as a result of completing the assignment task. In addition to being clear, the goals for this assignment focused on having students learn important academic skills: writing persuasively and supporting their statements with examples from a text. For these reasons, this assignment received the highest score for this dimension.

Applying Complex Thinking Skills: Analyzing and Interpreting a Text

Students were asked to write an evaluation of a book they had read and explain why that book would be a good choice for a seventh grader. The teacher also prompted them to include a lot of examples from the text. As evidenced in the example of student work, however, students did not articulate academically substantive criteria for reviewing their books. "Cool," for example, is not a rigorous criterion for judging the quality of a book. Students also were not held accountable for writing persuasively (one of the teacher's learning goals) and convincing the reader that the book they chose was a good one for a seventh grader. Instead, students mostly wrote essays that provided a very basic description of the events in the story they read. For this reason, this assignment received a 2 for the application of complex thinking skills. If students had applied more rigorous criteria in their evaluations and constructed an argument for why the book they read was or was not good (e.g., they wrote that the descriptions were vivid, the characters were real, the dialogue was believable, and the plot was unpredictable), then this assignment would have received a higher score for this dimension.

Developing Clear and Rigorous Criteria to Assess Students' Work

The rubric the teacher used to assess the quality of the students' work contains a great deal of information about the teacher's expectations for high-quality work. For example, the rubric makes clear that to receive a high score on this assignment, students needed to clearly state the criterion upon which they are judging the quality of the books they had read. Additionally, the rubric includes a focus on complex thinking skills (stating a criteria for evaluation and supporting reasons with evidence from the text) as well as writing conventions (e.g., grammar, punctuation, and spelling). For these reasons, this assignment received the highest score, a 4, for this dimension.

Communicating the Criteria for
High-Quality Work to Students

The teacher reported that she did not share models of high-quality work with students in advance of their completing this assignment and did not provide them with a copy of her rubric, though she did discuss the criteria with students in class before the assignment was due. This assignment, therefore, illustrates a score of 2 for this dimension.

Providing Clear and Rigorous Written Assignment Directions

The teacher did not provide students with written directions for this assignment.

Providing Content-Specific Feedback
on Drafts of Students' Work

Students wrote two drafts of their essays, a preliminary draft that was corrected by the teacher and another student, and a final draft. The feedback students received from the teacher focused almost exclusively on correcting students' language use (specifically, word choices) and writing mechanics. The result was that the final draft was improved in terms of language conventions but showed little improvement in its content. For this reason, this assignment received a 2 for the quality of the feedback given to students on drafts of their written work.

Aligning the Goals for Student Learning
With the Assignment Task

This assignment was scored a 2 for the alignment between the learning goals and the assignment task. This is because the teacher's goals, that students write a five-paragraph essay and "develop their skills at writing persuasively and supporting their answers with examples from the text," were only partially realized in the assignment task. Students wrote five-paragraph evaluations and included examples from the text in their writing. As evidenced in students' work, however, the assignment did not support development of students' persuasive writing skills by having them state their evaluation criteria and then show how the book did or did not live up to these standards.

Aligning the Grading Criteria
With the Goals for Student Learning

The learning goals—that students write a five-paragraph essay, develop their persuasive writing skills, and support their answers with examples from the text—were represented in the criteria used to grade students' work. Students were assessed on their five-paragraph essay writing, statement of evaluation criteria, and the quality of the evidence they used to support their arguments. For this reason, this assignment illustrates the highest score, a 3, for this dimension.

Summary of the Strengths and Weaknesses
of the Book Evaluation Assignment

The strengths of this assignment were that the teacher had clear goals that focused on important academic learning. Additionally, her grading criteria were aligned with her learning goals and focused on assessing complex thinking skills. This assignment would have been strengthened if the teacher's learning goals had been more fully realized in the design of the assignment task, however. Specifically, the assignment would have been improved if students had been given more guidance and support for constructing rigorous criteria by which to judge their book and for using evidence to support their evaluations. The assignment also would have been strengthened if students had read books that contained more substantive academic content. Sharing the grading criteria with students in advance of their completing the assignment and providing them with models of high-quality work might also have improved students' opportunity to produce high-quality work.

DESCRIPTIVE ESSAY: SEVENTH GRADE

For this assignment students read *Beowulf: A New Telling* by Robert Nye and wrote an essay describing Beowulf's heroic qualities. The teacher's learning goals for this assignment were "reading comprehension and applying the format of a five-paragraph essay." The students produced a total of three drafts for this assignment. On the first, students received some content-level feedback from the teacher that focused mostly on having students add examples from the text to support their statements and restate their theses in their conclusion. On the second draft, the teacher focused mostly on correcting students' language use, grammar, punctuation, and spelling. The following is an excerpt from the final draft of a student's essay:

Beowulf: A Hero

Beowulf was a very good person. He was strong, patient and brave. Beowulf was not greedy or ambitious, that is why he was a hero.

Beowulf showed how brave he was in many ways. He was brave in the story because he had lots of bees. Even though they stung him and nearly made him blind he still had hives of bees out in the field. Beowulf also killed all the monsters. He killed Grendel and She. For those things he did, I think that makes him very brave.

To assess the quality of students' work the teacher used the following criteria:

- content
- five-paragraph essay format
- correct grammar, spelling, and punctuation

The teacher reported that she did not provide students with a copy of these criteria or models of high-quality work in advance of their completing their assignments but that she did discuss these criteria with students in class.

The teacher's written directions given to students for this assignment were as follows:

Beowulf Essay

Write a five-paragraph essay describing the qualities that make Beowulf a hero. Remember to:

1. Make a graphic organizer to organize your thinking
2. Include the graphic organizer with your first draft when you turn it in
3. Apply the correct format for a five-paragraph essay
4. Use lots of examples from the story to support your ideas

Engaging With Substantive Academic Content

The text for this assignment illustrates the highest score, a 3, for this dimension. It tells the story of an ancient hero (Beowulf) and his quest against evil. This version of the story has been rewritten from its original form so that it is much more accessible to younger students. Besides being an interpretation of a literary classic, *Beowulf: A New Telling* is a good choice for seventh graders because it contains a multidimensional hero and interesting thematic material regarding the nature of good and evil.

Setting Clear and Rigorous Goals for Student Learning

This assignment received a 2 for the clarity and rigor of the learning goals. The first goal, reading comprehension, is quite general and does not specify the particular reading comprehension skills the teacher wanted students to learn as a result of completing the assignment task. The second half of the teacher's goals, that students apply "the format of a five-paragraph essay," are also nonspecific in terms of student learning. For example, it is not clear what particular aspect of five-paragraph essay writing the teacher wanted students to practice or learn through the completion of the assignment activity. For example, did she want students to learn to write more convincing thesis statements? Or hone their ability to use evidence to support an argument? If these goals had been more explicit, and if they had included a stronger focus on higher-level skills, then this assignment would have received a higher score for this dimension.

Applying Complex Thinking Skills:
Analyzing and Interpreting a Text

For this assignment students wrote a five-paragraph essay describing the qualities that made Beowulf a hero. This assignment required students to construct knowledge and apply analytic skills and so received a 3 for this dimension. As illustrated in the excerpt from a student's essay, however, students did not cite a great deal of evidence from the text in support of their position or go into much depth in their analysis. This is true even in the essays the teacher considered to be of high quality for the class. If students had used more evidence from the text to support their analyses or engaged in a more rigorous analysis (e.g., described how the hardships encountered by Beowulf contributed to his development as a hero) then this assignment likely would have received the highest score, a 4, for the application of complex thinking skills.

Developing Clear and Rigorous Criteria to Assess Students' Work

The teacher's criteria were, as in the case of the learning goals, very broad and nonspecific and contained hardly any information that could help students improve the quality of their work. It is not clear what the teacher was looking for in terms of high-quality "content" or what she considered to be a high-quality application of the five-paragraph essay format. Because these criteria were so general, this assignment received a 2 for this dimension. This assignment would have received a higher score for this dimension if the teacher had outlined what she was looking for in terms of content and format (e.g., factual accuracy, clear thesis statement, strong topic sentences with supporting sentences, restatement of thesis in conclusion, and convincing reasons why Beowulf was a hero), and if the criteria had made clear to students what they would need to do to produce a high-quality, versus a lower-quality, essay.

Communicating the Criteria for High-Quality Work to Students

This assignment illustrates a score of 2 for this dimension because the teacher reported that she discussed in class her criteria for grading student work but did not provide students with a copy of her criteria or models of high-quality work in advance of their completing the assignment.

Providing Clear and Rigorous Written Assignment Directions

As shown before, the written directions given to students for this assignment were not especially detailed and provided only basic information to students about what they needed to do to complete the task. The directions contained almost no information that would help students earn a good grade on their essays. For this reason, this assignment was considered to illustrate a 2 for this dimension.

Providing Content-Specific Feedback on Drafts of Students' Work

The students produced a total of three drafts for this assignment. On the first, students received some content-level feedback from the teacher that focused mostly on having students add examples from the text to support their statements and restate their theses in their conclusion. On the second draft, the teacher focused mostly on correcting students' language use, grammar, punctuation, and spelling. Because the students did receive content-level feedback on early drafts, this assignment received the highest score, a 3, for this dimension, though the students' work could have benefited from additional iterations or guidance on adding more story details and strengthening the language.

Aligning the Goals for Student Learning With the Assignment Task

As described earlier, the teacher's learning goals for this assignment, "reading comprehension and applying the format of a five-paragraph essay," were extremely general. Many different types of assignments could have fulfilled these goals. The learning goals and the task for this assignment, therefore, were aligned at a very general level only and so received a 2 for this dimension.

Aligning the Grading Criteria With the Goals for Student Learning

The teacher's learning goals, "reading comprehension and applying the format of a five-paragraph essay" and the grading criteria are both very nonspecific. It is not clear what the teacher was looking for in terms of the students learning "reading comprehension" skills, or what she was looking for in the "content" of students' essays. The teacher's grading criteria included a focus on the five-paragraph essay format, however, and this is reflected in the learning goals. For this reason, the learning goals and grading criteria were considered to be only partially aligned, and so this assignment received a 2 for this dimension.

Summary of the Strengths and Weaknesses of the Descriptive Essay Assignment

The text used for this assignment was very strong. Additionally, the teacher had the students write an interesting multiparagraph essay, which required them to apply some analysis skills and think about the story beyond its surface-level details. The teacher also provided the students with some content-level feedback on early drafts of their work. This assignment would have been even stronger if the teacher had had more specific learning goals that were realized in the assignment task. Additionally, the assignment and the quality of student work might have been improved if the teacher had developed her grading criteria (both the clarity and the content) and communicated her expectations more specifically with students in advance of their completion of their essays. In other words, if the teacher had made her expectations clearer to students about what she was looking for in terms of the quality of the content of their essays, and if students had received more extensive feedback about the content of their essays (especially on early drafts of their work). Providing students with good models of student work and detailed assignment directions also might have guided students to produce higher-quality essays.

COMPREHENSION QUESTIONS: TENTH GRADE

For this assignment students read *Of Mice and Men* by John Steinbeck and wrote one- or two-sentence responses to a series of comprehension questions. The teacher's learning goals for this assignment were, "I wanted the students to learn to think critically about what they read."

The following is an example of student work for this assignment considered to be of high quality for the class:

Of Mice and Men

Why does Curley pick on Lennie? He doesn't like guys who are big.

What does Curley's wife say is the reason she came out to the bunkhouse? She said she was looking for Curley.

What does Lennie say about Curley's wife? Lennie says that she is pretty and nice.

What is the jerkline skinner's name? What does he look like? His name was Slim and he was tall and thin.

What is Lennie's last name? Why did his name make Carlson laugh? His last name is Small and Carlson laughed because Lennie is big.

To assess the quality of the students' work, the teacher used the following criteria:

High-quality student work had thorough and accurate answers, medium-quality student work had less thorough answers but were still basically correct; low-quality student work had many errors or incomplete answers.

These criteria were not shared with students in advance of their completing the assignment, and students did not receive models of high-quality work. Students also did not receive written assignment directions.

Engaging With Substantive Academic Content

The text students read for this assignment, *Of Mice and Men*, is a classic work of American fiction. This story contains complex characters and insight into the life of migrant workers during the Depression. Because of the rich content of the story—both thematic and sociohistorical—this assignment received the highest score, a 3, for this dimension.

Setting Clear and Rigorous Goals for Student Learning

The learning goals for this assignment—"I wanted the students to learn to think critically about what they read"—were not very specific and did not include having students master academically rigorous content or skills. It is not clear what type of critical-thinking skills the teacher intended students to develop through completing the assignment task or how the assignment task would support these learning goals. For this reason, this assignment was considered to illustrate a 2 for this dimension.

Applying Complex Thinking Skills: Analyzing and Interpreting a Text

Although the text students read for this assignment was excellent, the assignment task received the lowest score, a 1, for the application of complex thinking skills. The comprehension questions students answered guided students to recall basic, isolated facts about surface-level features of the story. These questions did not prompt students to gain a deeper insight into the content of the story or even build a coherent representation of the story's events. Additionally, students were guided to produce only very short responses (one or two sentences). This assignment would have received a higher score for this dimension if it had fostered students' engagement with the deeper-level content of the story and encouraged them to use evidence from the text to support their assertions; for example, if students had written about George and Lenny's complex, symbiotic friendship, the themes of alienation and powerlessness that run through the story, or even the story's historical context.

Developing Clear and Rigorous Criteria to Assess Students' Work

The grading criteria for this assignment did not specify what the teacher considerd to be "thorough" answers. For this reason, this assignment received a low score, a 2, for this dimension. This assignment would have received a higher score for this dimension if the teacher had been explicit about what she was looking for in terms of the quality and content of students' answers.

Communicating the Criteria for High-Quality Work to Students

The teacher reported that she did not discuss these assessment criteria with students in advance of their completing the assignment. This assignment, therefore, received a 1 for this dimension.

Providing Clear and Rigorous Written Assignment Directions

This dimension was not scored, since the teacher did not provide written directions to students for how to complete the assignment.

Providing Content-Specific Feedback on Drafts of Students' Work

The students produced only one written draft for this assignment, so this dimension was not assessed.

Aligning the Goals for Student Learning With the Assignment Task

The learning goal for this assignment, that students "learn to think critically" about the text, was not furthered through the assignment task. Recalling basic, isolated facts about the story does not prompt students to think critically about it. For this reason this assignment received the lowest score, a 1, for the alignment of the learning goals with the assignment task.

Aligning the Grading Criteria With the Goals for Student Learning

The learning goal that students "learn to think critically about what they read" also was not reflected in the grading criteria that focused on students having "thorough" and "accurate" answers. For this reason, this assignment received a 1 for the alignment of the grading criteria with the goals for student learning.

Summary of the Strengths and Weaknesses of the Comprehension Question Assignment

The strength of this assignment lies primarily in the teacher's choice of a text. *Of Mice and Men* is an excellent, grade-appropriate choice for tenth-grade students. While the teacher's learning goal for this assignment was that students learn to think critically about this text, this goal was not reflected in what students were asked to do. Students answered basic recall questions that did not guide them to engage with the book's rich thematic content, and they produced only very short responses with little or no details from the story. The grading criteria also did not focus on the content of students' responses or the development of complex (or critical) thinking skills or provide students with a great deal of information about how to successfully complete the task. This assignment would have been stronger if the teacher had focused on her learning goals and created an assignment that supported students to develop their analysis and interpretation skills and produce more elaborated responses that included examples and evidence from the text. This assignment also would have been stronger if the teacher had focused her assessment criteria on the attainment of more complex (critical) thinking skills and communicated her expectations for high-quality work to students in advance of their completing the assignment.

ANALYTIC ESSAY: TENTH GRADE

For this assignment, students read *The Scarlet Letter* by Nathaniel Hawthorne and wrote a multiparagraph essay about the author's use of symbolism in the story. The teacher's goals for this assignment were as follows:

> I wanted students to demonstrate their critical thinking skills by identifying and describing a specific literary device in the story (the author's use of symbolism) and show how the symbols furthered the story's action. I also wanted them to use concrete examples from the story to support their responses.

The following is an excerpt from a student's essay, considered by the teacher to be of medium quality for the class:

The Scarlet Letter

Symbols are very important to a story. They change the meaning of the plot. They are small, but essential to the story and its content.

One of the most obvious symbols in *The Scarlet Letter* is the name of Hester's daughter.Her name is Pearl and she symbolizes that she is Hester's treasure. Pearl also is not only a symbol of Hester's sin but of the priest's sin too . . . Since Pearl was made from a sin she is defiant of others. "It was as if she had been made afresh, out of new element, and must perforce be permitted to live her own life, and be a law unto herself without her eccentricities being reckoned to her for a crime." She doesn't follow society, only God.

To assess the quality of students' work the teacher used a five-point rubric. This is the criteria for the highest score, a 5:

- Student identifies and describes three symbols from the story and shows how these symbols further the story's action
- Several text references/quotes
- Analysis is precise, engages with underlying meaning and subtle nuances of the text
- Shows command of style and writing conventions

The teacher reported that she shared this rubric with students in advance of their completing the assignment and provided them with models of high-quality work as well. The written directions provided to students for this assignment were as follows:

Scarlet Letter Essay

The purpose of your essay is to describe the author's use of symbols in *The Scarlet Letter* and how these symbols worked to enhance and support the story's plot. Your essay should be at least five paragraphs long and include supporting quotes and examples from the story.

In your essays remember to provide three detailed examples of how Nathaniel Hawthorne used symbols in *The Scarlet Letter*. For each example include the following:

- A description of the symbol and what it represented in the story
- Its thematic importance or function in the story

Remember that your essay should include an introductory paragraph with a thesis statement and a strong conclusion that recapitulates the ideas expressed in the introduction.

Students wrote two drafts of their essays and received comments pertaining to the mechanics of their writing on the first draft and content-level comments on their completed (final) draft.

Engaging With Substantive Academic Content

As with the previous assignment, the text chosen for this assignment is rich in thematic grist and symbolism. This book also deals with interesting moral issues relating to the intersection of religion and society and therefore is an excellent, challenging selection for tenth grade. For these reasons this assignment received the highest score, a 3, for the rigor of the text.

Setting Clear and Rigorous Goals for Student Learning

The learning goals for this assignment are quite explicit about the specific skills the teacher intends for the students to practice through completing the assignment: identifying and describing the author's use of symbols and showing with detailed evidence from the text how these furthered the story's action. These goals also focus on getting students to develop their analytic skills and look beyond the surface-level feature of a story. For these reasons, this assignment received the highest score, a 4, for this dimension.

Applying Complex Thinking Skills: Analyzing and Interpreting a Text

This assignment also received the highest score, a 4, for the application of complex thinking skills. Students were asked to write a multiparagraph essay in which they described the author's use of symbols in the text. This assignment gave students an opportunity to engage with the nuances of the story and to practice their analytical skills. This is evident in students' work—even student work that the teacher considered to be of medium, rather than high, quality for the class. For example, the student whose work is excerpted identified the author's use of symbols (the name of Hester's daughter) and supported her assertions with examples from the text. Although her writing could have been better organized and included more detail from the story to illustrate how these symbols related to the thematic content, it is clear that the student was learning and thinking about the symbolic meaning of the story.

Developing Clear and Rigorous Criteria to Assess Students' Work

To assess students' work, the teacher used a rubric that clearly set out what students needed to do to receive a high grade on the task. This rubric had the potential to provide students with a great deal of information about the teacher's expectations for the task and focused as well on the students' attainment of complex thinking skills (the quality of the students' analyses) and use of evidence from the text to support their responses. For these reasons, this assignment illustrates the highest score, a 4, for this dimension.

Communicating the Criteria for High Quality Work to Students

The teacher reported that she shared her grading criteria (the rubric) with students in advance of their completing the assignment and provided them with models of high-quality work as well. This assignment, therefore, received a 3 for this dimension. To receive the highest score, a 4, the teacher also would have allowed students to apply the rubrics to assess their own work.

Providing Clear and Rigorous Written Assignment Directions

The teacher communicated her expectations for high-quality work to the students in the form of detailed written assignment directions. As shown previously, these directions supported students' efforts by providing them with guidelines for writing their essay and reminded them of what they needed to do, and include in their writing, to obtain a high grade. For this reason, this assignment received the highest score, a 3, for the clarity of the teacher's written assignment directions provided to students.

Providing Content-Specific Feedback on Drafts of Students' Work

Students wrote multiple drafts of their essays and received feedback on early drafts of their essays from other students in the class, not from the teacher. Instead the teacher supplied feedback to students on the *final* drafts of their essays. Although the teacher provided many insightful comments to students on the content of their writing, because the students did not receive these comments earlier they did not have the opportunity to use the teacher's feedback to revise their work. This is a lost opportunity for student learning. As described in Chapter 7, it is not clear whether or not students apply the comments they receive on final drafts of their essays toward improving their writing on the next assignment. Because students only received surface-level feedback (from peers) on earlier drafts of their essays, this assignment received a 2 for this dimension. If students had been given the chance to use the teacher's comments to revise their work, then this assignment would have received the highest score, a 3, for the quality of the written feedback provided to students.

Aligning the Goals for Student Learning With the Assignment Task

The teacher's learning goals for this assignment—that students identify and describe the symbols used in the story, show how the symbols were thematically important, and "support their answers with details from the text"—are specific and overlapped completely with the assignment task. Students were guided to identify and describe the symbols used in the story, describe the symbols' thematic importance, and use concrete examples from the story to support their responses. For this reason, this assignment illustrates the highest score, a 3, for this dimension.

Aligning the Grading Criteria With the Goals for Student Learning

The teacher's learning goals and her grading criteria were considered to be fully aligned and so received the highest score, a 3, for this dimension. The rubric used by the teacher overlapped with her learning goals. Students were assessed on their identification and description of three symbols in the story and how these symbols further the story's action. Students also were assessed on their use of evidence to support their assertions.

Summary of the Strengths and Weaknesses of the Analytic Essay Assignment

This is a strong assignment in many respects. The teacher's learning goals were clear and focused on academically rigorous content. These goals, that students identify the author's use of symbols and show with details from the text how these furthered the story's actions, also were fully aligned with the requirements of the assignment. This task supported students to develop their skills at analyzing and interpreting a text, and this was reflected in students' work. Students also read an academically substantive text and produced multiparagraph essays that contained evidence from the text to support their assertions. The grading criteria also were detailed and aligned with the teacher's learning goals. In short, the only true weakness of this assignment was that students did not have the opportunity to incorporate the teacher's feedback in their revisions. This was unfortunate, since the teacher's comments on final drafts of students' papers were quite insightful and focused on the content of students' ideas. If students had had a chance to use these comments to guide their revisions, then the quality of students' work likely would have been even stronger than it was.

APPENDIX: RUBRICS AND QUESTIONS TO GUIDE REFLECTION AND ANALYSIS

Engaging With Substantive Academic Content (Grist)

Level 1	Level 2	Level 3
The text does not contain sufficiently complex themes or ideas to support a meaningful response (e.g., the text has a very simple plot, one-dimensional characters, and straightforward dilemmas that have an obvious right or wrong answer).	The text contains some degree of thematic complexity but does not challenge students' thinking.	Students engage with substantive content. The text contains complex themes and ideas that support meaningful responses.

- Does the text read by students contain complex themes or ideas? For example, are students given insight into a character's inner thoughts? Does the story contain an interesting moral dilemma to which there is not necessarily an obvious right or wrong answer? Are the characters in the book multifaceted (i.e., display both positive and negative traits)?
- Does the text provide students with access to learning in other content areas? For example, do they have an opportunity to learn about life in other historical periods or about other cultures?

Setting Clear and Rigorous Goals for Student Learning

Level 1	Level 2	Level 3	Level 4
Goals are unclear and/or do not focus on students' comprehension of a text.	Goals are broadly stated and/or the goals focus on students attaining a surface-level understanding of a text.	Goals are clear in terms of what students are to learn from completing the assignment activity. At least some of the goals focus on students analyzing and interpreting a text (e.g., inferring major themes, comparing and contrasting, and applying an external criterion to evaluate a text).	Goals are clear in terms of what students are to learn as a result of completing the assignment task. At least some of the goals focus on students analyzing and interpreting a text (e.g., inferring major themes, comparing and contrasting, and applying an external criterion to evaluate a text) but in addition, using evidence from a text to support a position.

- What specific ideas or content from the text are students expected to learn as a result of completing this assignment?
- What writing skills are students expected to develop as a result of completing this assignment?
- Are the instructional goals clear and detailed?
- How do these goals fit with the standards for learning and instruction?
- Do at least some of the learning goals focus on having students analyze and interpret a text (e.g., inferring major themes, comparing and contrasting, and applying an external set of criteria to evaluate a text)?
- Do the learning goals include having students use evidence from the text to support their responses?

Applying Complex Thinking Skills: Analyzing and Interpreting a Text

Level 1	Level 2	Level 3	Level 4
The assignment task guides students (1) to recall isolated straightforward information or (2) to write on a topic that does not directly reference information from the text.	The assignment task guides students (1) to construct a basic summary of the text only or (2) to apply comprehension strategies at a surface level with little or no evidence from the text to support their responses.	The assignment task guides students to begin to analyze and interpret the text and support their responses with limited evidence from the text.	The assignment task guides students to fully analyze and interpret the text and support their responses with detailed evidence from the text.

- What skills do students need to apply to complete this assignment (e.g., recall of facts, summarization, evaluation, and analysis)?
- Did students need to have a thorough understanding of the events and interrelationship of events in the text to complete this assignment? Was this reflected in student work of high, medium, and low quality?
- Did students need to have a thorough understanding of the nonobvious features of the text (e.g., the theme, the message of the text, a character's motivation, literary symbolism, and historical context) to complete this assignment? Was this reflected in student work of high, medium, and low quality?
- Did the assignment guide students to support their responses with detailed evidence from the text? Was this reflected in student work of high, medium, and low quality?

Developing Clear and Rigorous Criteria to Assess Students' Work

Level 1	Level 2	Level 3	Level 4
Grading criteria are unclear and/or do not focus on students' comprehension of a text.	Grading criteria are broadly stated and/or criteria focus on students attaining a surface-level understanding of a text.	The grading criteria used to assess students' work are clear and somewhat elaborated. Levels of quality may be differentiated for each criterion, but little information is provided for what distinguishes between low, medium, and high work. At least some of the criteria focus on students analyzing and interpreting a text (e.g., inferring major themes, comparing and contrasting, and applying an external criterion to evaluate a text).	The grading criteria used to assess students' work are very clear and elaborated. Each dimension or criterion for the quality of students' work is clearly articulated. Additionally, varying degrees of success are clearly differentiated. At least some of the criteria focus on students analyzing and interpreting a text (e.g., inferring major themes, comparing and contrasting, and applying an external criterion to evaluate a text) and using evidence from a text to support a position.

- How clear and detailed are the criteria for grading students' work?
- Do these criteria contain enough information so that a student would know the expectations for work of high, medium, and low quality? Do these criteria contain enough information so that a student could improve their work if given the opportunity?
- Do at least some of the criteria for assessing the quality of students' work focus on having students analyze and interpret a text?
- Do at least some of the criteria for assessing the quality of students' work focus on the quality of the evidence students use to support their answers?

Communicating the Criteria for High-Quality Work to Students

Level 1	Level 2	Level 3	Level 4
Teacher does not share her criteria for assessing students' work in advance of their completing an assignment.	Teacher discusses the criteria for assessing students' work (e.g., scoring guide and rubric) with students in advance of their completing an assignment.	Teacher discusses the criteria for assessing students' work (e.g., scoring guide and rubric) with students in advance of their completing an assignment and provides students access to a written version of these criteria (e.g., a criteria chart and models of high-quality work).	Teacher discusses the criteria for assessing students' work (e.g., scoring guide and rubric) with students in advance of their completing an assignment and provides students access to a written version of these criteria. The students also are actively encouraged to apply the criteria to their own or a peer's work.

- Were the criteria for grading students' work discussed with them in class?
- Did students have access to a written version of the criteria (e.g., a criteria chart posted in a visible part of the classroom, or a copy of a rubric)?
- Did students have access to models of high-quality work that were linked to the grading criteria?
- Were students given the opportunity to apply these criteria to analyze their own (and/or a peer's) work?

Providing Clear and Rigorous Written Assignment Directions

Level 1	Level 2	Level 3
The assignment directions are nonspecific and provide little or no information to students regarding what they need to do to successfully complete the task.	The assignment directions are clear and provide general information to students regarding what they need to do, or include in their work, to successfully complete the task.	The assignment directions are clear and detailed and provide a great deal of information to students regarding what they need to do, or include in their work, to successfully complete the task.

- How detailed are the assignment directions?
- Do the assignment directions provide enough guidance to students with regard to what they would need to do, or include in their work, to be successful on this assignment?
- Do the directions include a focus on having students analyze and interpret a text?
- Do the directions include a focus on the quality of the evidence students use to support their answers?

Providing Content-Specific Feedback on Drafts of Students' Work

Level 1	Level 2	Level 3
Students did not receive comments on early drafts of their compositions. There was little or no guidance for revision.	Students received comments on early drafts of their compositions that focused on surface-level features of their writing (grammar, punctuation, spelling, and language use). Guidance for revision focused on improving the mechanics of students' writing.	Students received comments on early drafts of their compositions that focused on content of their writing (as well as surface-level features). Guidance for revision focused on improving the content of students' compositions, as well as the mechanics of their writing.

- Did students receive feedback on the content of their writing on early drafts of their compositions and thus have the opportunity to incorporate these comments in their revisions?
- If the assignment required students to produce multiple drafts of their written work, did students receive written comments that focused on the content of their writing in addition to corrections in their grammar, spelling, punctuation, and language use?
- Did students incorporate the feedback they received on early drafts of their writing in their later drafts?

Aligning the Goals for Student Learning With the Assignment Task

Level 1	Level 2	Level 3
The learning goals and the assignment task are not aligned.	The learning goals and the assignment task are partially aligned or are aligned at a very general level.	The learning goals and the assignment task are fully aligned. Goals are clear and specific, and these goals are furthered through the lesson activity.

- Were the goals for student learning furthered in the assignment task? For example, if the goal was for students to develop their analytical thinking skills, were students required to apply analytical skills to complete the assignment?
- How specific was the alignment between the goals for student learning and the assignment task?

Aligning the Grading Criteria With the Goals for Student Learning

Level 1	Level 2	Level 3
The grading criteria and the learning goals are not aligned.	The grading criteria and the learning goals are partially aligned or are aligned at a very general level.	The grading criteria and the learning goals are detailed and fully aligned.

- Were the goals for student learning reflected in the grading criteria? For example, if the goal was for students to develop their analytical thinking skills, were students assessed on the quality of their analyses?
- How specific was the alignment between the goals for student learning and the grading criteria?

REFERENCES

Applebee, A. N. (1984). *Contexts for learning to write: Studies of secondary school instruction.* Norwood, NJ: Ablex.

Aschbacher, P. R. (1999). *Developing indicators of classroom practice to monitor and support school reform* (CSE Tech. Rep. No. 513). Los Angeles: University of California, National Center for Research on Evaluation, Standards and Student Testing.

Beck, I. L., & McKeown, M. G. (2001). Text talk: Capturing the benefits of read-aloud experiences for young children. *The Reading Teacher, 55*, 10–20.

Beck, I. L., McKeown, M. G., Hamilton, R. L., & Kucan, L. (1997). *Questioning the author: An approach for enhancing student engagement with text.* Newark, DE: International Reading Association.

Beason, L. (1993). Feedback and revision in writing across the curriculum classes. *Research in the Teaching of English, 27*, 395–421.

Black, P., & Wiliam, D. (1998). Inside the black box: Raising standards through classroom assessment. *Phi Delta Kappan, 80*(2), 139–144.

Bloom, H. S. (1956). *Taxonomy of educational objectives.* Handbook I: Cognitive domain. New York: McKay.

Clare, L., & Aschbacher, P. (2001). Exploring the technical quality of using assignments and student work as indicators of classroom practice. *Educational Assessment, 7*(1), 39–59.

Cohen, D. K., McLaughlin, M. W., & Talbert, J. E. (Eds.). (1993). *Teaching for understanding: Challenges for policy and practice.* San Francisco: Jossey-Bass.

Covey, S. R. (1989). *The seven habits of highly effective people: Restoring the character ethic.* New York: Free Press.

Crosson, A., Junker, B. W., Matsumura, L. C., & Resnick, L. B. (2003, April). *Developing an instructional quality assessment.* Paper presented at the annual meeting of the American Educational Research Association, Chicago, IL.

Fuhrman, S. (1993). *Designing coherent education policy: Improving the system.* San Francisco: Jossey-Bass.

Gallimore, R., & Tharp, R. (2004). What a coach can teach a teacher 1975–2004: Reflections and reanalysis of John Wooden's teaching practices. *The Sport Psychologist,* 18(2), 119–137.

Goldenberg, C. (2004). *Successful school change: Creating settings to improve teaching and learning.* New York: Teachers College Press.

Hiebert, J., Gallimore, R., & Stigler, J. (2002). A knowledge base for the teaching profession: What would it look like, and how can we get one? *Educational Researcher,* 31(5), 3–15.

Hopman, M., & Glynn, T. (1988). Behavioral approaches to improving written expression. *Educational Psychology,* 8, 81–100.

Lieberman, A. (1994). Teacher development: Commitment and challenge. In P. Grimmet & J. Neufield (Eds.), *Teacher development and the struggle for authenticity* (15–30). New York: Teachers College Press.

Matsumura, L. C. (2002). *Principles of learning.* Institute for Learning University of Pittsburgh. Retrieved November 11, 2004, from http://www.instituteforlearning.org/pol3.html.

Matsumura, L. C., Garnier, H., Pascal, J., & Valdés, R. (2002). Measuring instructional quality in accountability systems: Classroom assignments and student achievement. *Educational Assessment,* 8(3), 207–229.

Matsumura, L. C., Patthey-Chavez, G. G., Valdés, R., & Garnier, H. (2002). Teacher feedback, writing assignment quality, and third-grade students' revision in lower- and higher-achieving urban schools. *Elementary School Journal,* 103, 3–26.

National Reading Panel. (2000). *Teaching children to read: An evidence based assessment of the scientific research literature on reading and implications for reading instruction.* Washington, DC: National Institute of Child Health and Human Development.

Newmann, F. M., Bryk, A. S., & Nagaoka, J. K. (2001). *Authentic intellectual work and standardized tests: Conflict or coexistence?* Chicago: Consortium on Chicago School Research.

Newmann, F., Marks, H. M., & Gamoran, A. (1996). Authentic pedagogy and student performance. *American Journal of Education,* 104(4), 280–313.

Onosoko, J. J. (1992, April). Exploring the thinking of thoughtful teachers. *Educational Leadership,* 49(7), 40–43.

Patthey-Chavez, G. G., Matsumura, L. C., & Valdés, R. (2004). Investigating the process approach to writing instruction in urban middle school classrooms. *Journal of Adolescent and Adult Literacy, 47*(6), 462–477.

Rogoff, B. (1992). *Apprenticeship in thinking.* New York: Oxford University Press.

Slavin, R., & Madden, N. (1989). What works for students at risk: A research synthesis. *Educational Leadership, 46*(5), 4–13.

Snow, C. (2002). *Reading for understanding: Toward an R&D program in reading comprehension.* Santa Monica, CA: RAND.

Storms, B. A., Riazantseva, A., & Gentile, C. (2000). Focusing in on content and communication (Writing assignments that work). *California English, 5*(4), 26–27.

Saunders, W., Goldenberg, C., & Hamann, J. (1992). Instructional conversations beget instructional conversations. *Teaching and Teacher Education, 8,* 199–218.

Stigler, J. W., & Hiebert, J. (1999). *The teaching gap: Best ideas from the world's teachers for improving education in the classroom.* New York: Free Press.

Vygotsky, L. S. (1978). *Mind in society: The development of higher psychological processes.* Cambridge, MA: Harvard University Press.

White, E. B. (1952) *Charlotte's Web.* New York: HarperCollins.

Wooden, J. R., with Steve Jamison (1997). *Wooden: A lifetime of observations and reflections on and off the court.* Lincolnwood, IL: Contemporary Books.

TEXTS READ BY STUDENTS

Angelou, M. (1996). *I know why the caged bird sings.* New York: Chelsea House Publishers.

Angelou, M. (1994). "Alone." In *The complete collected poems of Maya Angelou.* New York: Random House.

Applegate, K. (1999). *Two-timing Aisha.* New York: Avon Books.

Atwater, R., & Atwater, F. (1988). *Mr. Popper's penguins.* Boston: Little, Brown.

Blume, J. (1991). *Tales of a fourth grade nothing.* New York: Dell.

Bolt, R. (1988). *A man for all seasons.* New York: Samuel French, Inc.

Bontemps, A. (1996). "A Black Man Talks of Reaping." In *American negro poetry.* New York: Hill and Wang.

Bradbury, R. (1993). *Fahrenheit 451.* New York: Simon & Schuster.

Buck, P. (1973). *The big wave.* New York: J. Day Co.

Cisneros, S. (1994). *The house on Mango Street.* New York: Knopf.

Cleary, B. (1955). *Beezus and Ramona.* New York: Dell.

Clements, A. (1988). *Big Al.* Saxonville, MA: Picture Books Studio.

Cowan, C. (1997). *My life with the wave.* New York: Lothrop, Lee & Shepard Books.

Cummings, P. (1991). *Clean your room, Harvey Moon!* New York: Bradbury Press.

Curtis, C. P. (1995). *The Watsons go to Birmingham—1963.* New York: Delacorte Press.

Estes, E. (1971). *The hundred dresses.* San Diego: Harcourt Brace.

Fleischman, S. (1963). *By the great horn spoon.* Boston: Little, Brown.

Frank, A. (1995). *Ann Frank: The diary of a young girl.* New York: Doubleday.

Gilman Perkins, C. (1993). *The yellow wallpaper.* New Brunswick: Rutgers University Press.

Hawthorne, N. (1990). *The scarlet letter.* New York: Vintage.

Holman, F. (1992). *Slake's limbo.* New York: Scholastic.

Houston, G. (1993). *My great-aunt Arizona.* New York: Scholastic.

Houston, J. W. (1995). *Farewell to Manzanar: A true story of Japanese American experience during and after the World War II internment.* New York: Bantam Books.

Howe, D., & Howe, J. (1996). *Bunnicula: A rabbit-tale of mystery.* New York: Aladdin.

Keyes, D. (1975). *Flowers for Algernon.* New York: Bantam Books.

Miller, A. (1995). *The crucible.* New York: Penguin Books.

Myers, W. (1996). "The treasure of Lemon Brown." In Paul Zindel (Ed.), *The pigman: With related readings.* New York: Glencoe/McGraw Hill.

Nye, R. (1982). *Beowulf: A new telling.* New York: Dell.

Orwell, G. (2000). *1984.* New York: Harcourt.

Rodgers, M. (1999). *Freaky Friday.* New York: Harper Trophy.

Scieszka, J. (1999). *The true story of the three little pigs.* New York: Viking.

Shakespeare, W. (2000). *Romeo and Juliet.* New York: Penguin.

Shakespeare, W. (2000). *The tragedy of Julius Caesar.* New York: Penguin.

Silverstein, S. (1992). *The giving tree.* New York: HarperCollins.

Speare , E. G. (1986). *The witch of Blackbird Pond.* Boston: Houghton Mifflin.

Steinbeck, J. (1965). *Of mice and men.* New York: Modern Library.

Stevenson, R. L. (2000). *Treasure island.* New York: Scholastic.

West, T. (1999). *Pokemon the first movie: Mewtwo strikes back.* New York: Scholastic.

Williams, V. (1982). *A chair for my mother.* New York: Scholastic.

INDEX

Shakespeare, William, 11, 25, 38, 105

Silverstein, Shel, 31

Slake's Limbo, 70

Speare, Elizabeth George, 89

standards for learning and instruction, viii, xiii, 20

Stanford Test of Academic Achievement (SAT-9), xii. *See also* student achievement

Steinbeck, John, 32, 128

Stevenson, Robert Louis, 83

student achievement, viii, xi

Tales of a Fourth-Grade Nothing, 82

"The Three Little Pigs," 13

The Tragedy of Julius Caesar, 105

Treasure Island, 83

"The Treasure of Lemon Brown," 34–35

The True Story of the Three Little Pigs, 99

Two-Timing Aisha, 15

The Watsons Go to Birmingham— 1963, 114–16

West, Tracy, 119–20

White, E.B, 11

Williams, Vera B., 33–34

The Witch of Blackbird Pond, 89

Wooden, John, vii

World War I, 92

writing instruction, process approach to, 74

The Yellow Wallpaper, 41

Yep, Laurence, 12

ABOUT THE AUTHOR

Lindsay Clare Matsumura is a research associate at the University of Pittsburgh. Her research focuses on assessing instructional quality and tracing the influence of reform policies on classroom practice. She is married and has one son.

DATE DUE